SAINT
BENEDICT

BOOKS BY MARY FABYAN WINDEATT

A Series of Twenty Books

Stories of the Saints for Young People ages 10 to 100

THE CHILDREN OF FATIMA
And Our Lady's Message to the World

THE CURÉ OF ARS
The Story of St. John Vianney, Patron Saint of Parish Priests

THE LITTLE FLOWER
The Story of St. Therese of the Child Jesus

PATRON SAINT OF FIRST COMMUNICANTS
The Story of Blessed Imelda Lambertini

THE MIRACULOUS MEDAL
The Story of Our Lady's Appearances to St. Catherine Labouré

ST. LOUIS DE MONTFORT
The Story of Our Lady's Slave, St. Louis Mary Grignion De Montfort

SAINT THOMAS AQUINAS
The Story of "The Dumb Ox"

SAINT CATHERINE OF SIENA
The Story of the Girl Who Saw Saints in the Sky

SAINT HYACINTH OF POLAND
The Story of the Apostle of the North

SAINT MARTIN DE PORRES
The Story of the Little Doctor of Lima, Peru

SAINT ROSE OF LIMA
The Story of the First Canonized Saint of the Americas

PAULINE JARICOT
Foundress of the Living Rosary & The Society for the Propagation of the Faith

SAINT DOMINIC
Preacher of the Rosary and Founder of the Dominican Order

SAINT PAUL THE APOSTLE
The Story of the Apostle to the Gentiles

SAINT BENEDICT
The Story of the Father of the Western Monks

KING DAVID AND HIS SONGS
A Story of the Psalms

SAINT MARGARET MARY
And the Promises of the Sacred Heart of Jesus

SAINT JOHN MASIAS
Marvelous Dominican Gatekeeper of Lima, Peru

SAINT FRANCIS SOLANO
Wonder-Worker of the New World and Apostle of Argentina and Peru

BLESSED MARIE OF NEW FRANCE
The Story of the First Missionary Sisters in Canada

SAINT BENEDICT

THE STORY OF THE
FATHER OF THE WESTERN MONKS

By
Mary Fabyan Windeatt

Illustrated by
Donald Walpole, O.S.B.
MONK OF ST. MEINRAD'S ABBEY

TAN Books
An Imprint of Saint Benedict Press, LLC
Charlotte, North Carolina

Nihil Obstat: Arthur J. Scanlan, S.T.D.
      Censor Librorum

Imprimatur: ✠ Francis J. Spellman, D.D.
      Archbishop of New York
      New York
      August 5, 1943

ISBN: 978-0-89555-427-7

Library of Congress Catalog Card No.: 93-61378

Printed and bound in the United States of America.

TAN Books
An Imprint of Saint Benedict Press, LLC
Charlotte, North Carolina
2012

For
Reverend Benedict Brown, O.S.B.,
Pastor of St. Mary's Church,
Huntingburg, Indiana.

CONTENTS

ACKNOWLEDGMENTS

The author wishes to thank the Reverend Paschal Boland, O.S.B., of St. Meinrad's Abbey, St. Meinrad, Indiana, and Sister M. Therese, O.S.B., of the Academy of the Immaculate Conception, Ferdinand, Indiana, for their valuable aid in preparing this story of Saint Benedict.

ST. MAURUS   ST. BENEDICT   ST. PLACID

SAINT BENEDICT

Chapter 1

THE BOY WHO RAN AWAY

CYRILLA was worried. Young Master Benedict, whose parents had sent him to study in the schools of Rome, was losing interest in his work. Only last night he had said that he didn't want to be a leader in law or politics. He only wanted to be a hermit in a cave.

"The foolish boy!" thought Cyrilla, as she set about getting supper for Benedict and herself. "If he really wants to lead a holy life, why can't he enter a monastery? There are plenty of them here in Rome."

Cyrilla sat down before the open fireplace and scowled at a kettle of water that was almost ready to boil. She was a woman in her middle fifties, short and plump, with her dark hair already streaked with grey. For many years she had been with Benedict's family. First it had been just as a simple maid. Later, when Benedict and his twin sister were born, she had been chosen to be their nurse.

"I was happy then," she thought. "I liked living in that little town of Nursia. But here in Rome things are so different. So much noise and dirt!"

1

There was a sudden sound of footsteps outside. The door opened and Cyrilla looked up. Young Master Benedict stood on the threshold. Eagerly, she scanned his face.

"Well?" she asked hopefully, but her heart sank even as she spoke. There was the same light in the boy's dark eyes. It was easy to see that he had not given up the idea of being a hermit.

"I told the schoolmaster I wouldn't be coming back any more. Please don't be cross, Cyrilla. There wasn't anything else I could do."

The woman got to her feet. "But Master Benedict! Your father's going to be so angry if you don't finish your education! After all, he's made so many fine plans. Why can't you wait until you're older before taking any such step as this?"

Benedict smiled. "I'm seventeen," he said gently. "Boys that age are old enough to go to war. Even to marry. But I . . . I just want to serve God. Surely you can understand that?"

The woman shook her head wearily. "I'll be blamed for all this," she murmured. "Just wait and see. Your father sent me here to Rome to be your housekeeper. What will he say when he hears I've let you run away from school? Ah, Master Benedict, you're going to break my heart!"

There was no doubt about the way Cyrilla felt. Benedict looked at her uneasily. He didn't want to hurt anyone, much less this kindly woman who had been his nurse since childhood. Yet what could he do? Rome, the great city where so many people spent their days trying to be rich and powerful, was not to his liking. He himself longed for the quiet of the countryside, for some small cave where he could spend his days in prayer.

"Don't worry," he said kindly. "I've heard that a hermit's life is really very healthy. Lots of fresh air, sunshine, simple food . . ."

"And cold winds, rain and snow! Master Benedict, you know you're not used to such things. Why, you'd die of the hardship within a month!"

"Not unless it was the Will of God, Cyrilla. Remember how He looks after everyone on this earth, even the birds and the flowers in the fields?"

Cyrilla sniffed. "If you're going off to be a hermit, it won't be by yourself," she declared. "I'll go with you and see that you don't starve to death."

The boy laughed. "But a hermit has to live alone, Cyrrilla, even if it is hard! That's the whole point to the life. A hermit cuts himself off from the world, from friends and all the usual comforts, so he can belong more wholly to God."

The kettle was boiling furiously now. Cyrilla went over and removed it from the fire. "You're going to be a different kind of hermit," she said firmly. "You're going to have someone to cook your meals and mend your clothes."

It was a few days later that Benedict and Cyrilla left Rome and headed eastward into the hill country. They had no real destination, save that the boy still had his mind set on living in a cave. When they had gone far enough, he said, they would surely come across some such place.

"I still think it's a foolish idea, going off like this

"THEY HAD NO REAL DESTINATION, SAVE THAT THE BOY STILL HAD HIS MIND SET ON LIVING IN A CAVE."

into the wilderness," muttered Cyrilla. "How do you know there aren't wild beasts in these woods? Or even thieves and murderers?"

Benedict smiled and shaded his eyes against the burning sun. "If there are, God will protect us from them," he said simply. "All we have to do is trust in Him."

faith

Of course trust in God was built on faith in Him. Faith! The boy liked the sound of that word. It was something that all the saints possessed in abundance. It enabled one to "see" beyond this world to the things of God. Once he was a hermit, he would try to increase his faith. He would try very hard to pray well, to find God in his own soul, to honor and love Him for all His goodness.

"It's going to be a wonderful life!" he thought. "I won't have to worry about being a success in the world, only about getting to Heaven and praying that all my friends and relatives get there, too."

But as the hours passed, Benedict became a bit worried. Cyrilla did not complain, but he could see she was growing tired.

"We'll stop for a while," he suggested kindly. "After all, we don't have to find a cave today, Cyrilla. It may take quite a while before we come across the right place."

The woman shook her head. "Let's keep on going, Master Benedict. This is such a dreadfully wild looking country."

Time passed, and the sun began to sink behind the hills. The sky turned from rosy pink to lavender, then to a deep purple. Presently it was night, with a million bright stars winking down on the lonely mountain road. Fireflies glittered among the trees. A soft wind stirred the tall grass, and somewhere in the distance a nightingale began to sing.

Benedict smiled. Cyrilla was too tired to care about the loveliness of the scene before them. She could scarcely drag one foot after the other.

"We'll spend the night under that big pine tree," the boy thought. "Surely no harm will come to us."

As he finished preparing a place for the two of them, he saw that Cyrilla was nearly asleep, her head heavy upon the little satchel of belongings she had brought. He smiled again as he settled down to keep watch over his faithful companion. In a way it was good to be adrift like this. It gave one a chance to rely completely on the providence of God.

The next day was clear and cloudless and Benedict and Cyrilla were up very early. The boy was still confident that he wanted to lead a hermit's life, but he could not help feeling worried about his companion. Cyrilla was not a young woman. Walking so many miles yesterday had been too much for her, and Benedict realized that something would have to be done. Either they would have to find a cave very soon or else make their way to some village.

"I don't want to be a nuisance," Cyrilla muttered, "but I can't keep on much longer, Master Benedict. My feet are so sore!"

The boy nodded. "All right. We'll go slowly for the rest of the morning. By the time night comes, I'm pretty sure we'll have found some good place to stay."

Benedict was right. Late that afternoon they glimpsed the spire of a little church. There were houses, too, and other signs that people were living in the neighborhood.

"Thanks be to God!" cried Cyrilla, as she stopped to gaze at a thin line of smoke rising from a chimney. "Master Benedict, you've no idea how glad I am to see this place!"

Chapter 2

A BROKEN SIEVE

ENFIDE was a Christian settlement, some thirty-five miles from Rome. Having explained their troubles, Benedict and Cyrilla were warmly welcomed by the people.

"Of course you may stay here until you're rested," they said. "Travelers are always welcome."

In his heart Benedict gave thanks to God. Enfide might be a poor spot, but everyone was kind. Already Cyrilla had made friends with the women-folk who were looking after her.

"But I mustn't forget why I left Rome," the boy warned himself. "It was not to live in comfort, among friends, but to spend my days in prayer for those who will not pray for themselves. Dear Lord, help me to find some lonely spot in these hills where I can begin my new life!"

Cyrilla had other ideas, however. "Why don't we stay here?" she asked one morning. "Ah, Master Benedict, you could serve God just as well in Enfide as in some damp cave. You're strong and well educated. The people here need a young man like you."

Benedict smiled. Poor faithful Cyrilla! Certainly

God had never given her a vocation to be a hermit. She saw only the hardships of the life, not its beauties.

"There are others who need me, too," he said gently. "You see, I want to spend my life praying for people who don't bother to pray for themselves. But you—well, I think God means you for some other work."

The woman looked up quickly. "I won't ever leave you, Master Benedict. Didn't I promise your father the day we left Nursia that I would care for you as though you were my own son? Ah, that's one promise I'll never break. I'll follow you wherever you go."

Benedict smiled. "You're a good friend," he said gently. "May God bless you for all your kindness."

As time passed, Cyrilla became more attached than ever to the new friends she had made. Knowing this, Benedict felt that soon he would go off to be a hermit by himself, as he had planned in the beginning. Each day he visited the local church and begged for light and courage to start his new life.

"Dear Lord," he prayed, "Cyrilla could never be happy as a hermit. That life is for me. Please look after her when I'm gone. And after my parents and my twin sister, back in Nursia. Bless us all, and help us to do Your holy Will. Amen."

He was returning from church one day, pondering how to break the news that soon he would be leaving Enfide, when he heard someone crying. It was Cyrilla, deeply upset because she had just broken an earthenware sieve.

"What am I going to do?" she moaned, as Benedict hastened to her. "I borrowed that sieve only this morning. And the woman who owns it has been so good to me, Master Benedict. So very good!"

Benedict looked at the sieve. It was broken in halves. Of course it could be mended, but the break would still show.

"Never mind," he told the weeping woman. "Let me have the two pieces. Perhaps I can think of some way . . ."

Cyrilla shook her head. "No one can fix it!" she sobbed. "I'd better go and tell the owner what I did. Oh, Master Benedict, why was I so clumsy?"

Benedict did not answer, but took the two earthenware fragments and left the room. Poor Cyrilla! She was making quite a fuss about the sieve. But why not? The owner was a poor woman. Probably the sieve she had lent Cyrilla was the best one she had.

When he was finally alone in his room, Benedict knelt down. "Dear Lord, be good enough to listen to me," he prayed. "Here is a little sieve that is broken. Will You mend it quickly, so that Cyrilla may be happy again? Will You show this village Your great power, so that everyone may love You even more than they have done?"

There were other words that Benedict said, words of praise and honor. In fact, he soon forgot about the broken sieve entirely, so wrapped up was he in the thought that God is everything and mankind only the creation of His love. But when he arose from his knees, he saw his prayer had been heard. The sieve was whole again. There was not the slightest sign of the place where it had been broken.

"Thank You," he murmured. "Always You are ready to help people when they have faith in You, when they act like little children speaking to a kindly father."

Cyrilla, though, was not satisfied with such a simple explanation. In fact, she was beside herself with excitement when she saw that the sieve was really in one piece again.

"Why, it's a miracle!" she cried. "Master Benedict, you've worked a miracle, just like the saints did!"

Benedict shook his head. "No miracle, Cyrilla. Only God has so much power. But He did listen to my poor prayers. Now you can return the sieve to its owner with a clear conscience."

Cyrilla's face was shining. "Just wait until people hear what you've done, Master Benedict! I've often tried to tell them what a holy life you lead. Now they'll think you're even better than I said!"

When Cyrilla had gone to show the mended sieve to its owner, Benedict thought hard. There was no telling what would take place in people's minds, once they had heard the story of the sieve. Cyrilla had always been fond of him. Even though she didn't approve of his wanting to be a hermit, secretly she was proud that he was not afraid to lead such a hard life. Now, probably, she would spread the word that he was nothing less than a saint.

"This is the time for me to leave Enfide," he

thought. "Cyrilla's friends will look after her. She'll
be quite happy in this little village. But I . . . I
couldn't bear to be thought of as a wonderworker.
Dear Lord, show me where to go. And quickly,
please!"

Enfide was such a small place that Benedict was
out of sight of the houses and church in only a few
minutes. He was sorry to leave in such a fashion,
but he knew God would let Cyrilla and her new
friends understand.

"I'm really going to be a hermit after all," he
thought. "This is the day I start being useful to
others."

The boy walked briskly along the winding road.
All about him were trees and bushes, but never a
sign of a human being. Occasionally a flock of
crows burst out of the woods, their black wings
glistening in the sunlight. Benedict watched them
go happily. Soon birds and other wild creatures
would be his only companions. That was the way
things were, when one was a hermit.

"But I still need a place to live in," he thought.
"Where is a nice cave, I wonder?"

He had walked about three miles when he saw a
man, dressed in a long grey robe, coining out of the
woods ahead of him. The stranger had a flowing
beard that gave him a rather wild appearance. On
his arm he carried a basket, half full of freshly
picked herbs. He turned as Benedict approached,
and the boy saw that the beard hid a kindly face.

"You are looking for the monastery, my son?"

Benedict shook his head and hurried to explain

"I AM VERY ANXIOUS TO BEGIN
A LIFE WHOLLY GIVEN TO GOD."

his presence. He was not looking for a monastery, but for a cave where he could be a hermit.

"Perhaps you know of some such place?" he asked.

The man smiled. "I am a monk, my son. I am called Romanus. I have lived in yonder monastery for many years."

"Then you must know this place well?"

"Very well."

Benedict sighed with relief. "Then tell me, good Romanus, where I may find a hermit's cave. I want to begin a life wholly given to God."

Romanus eyed the boy shrewdly. Undoubtedly here was a lad of good birth and of more than ordinary promise. Probably he had run away from a comfortable life in the belief that God wished him to become a hermit. But did the lad realize the difficulties of the solitary life? Did he have the necessary strength to live on herbs and wild berries?

"My son, I've seen many hermits in my day. They were good men, of much prayer and sacrifice. But you . . . why, you're a mere boy! Of course holy zeal is a fine thing, but perhaps, in some cases . . ."

Benedict smiled. The monk's words were familiar. Cyrilla had used them over and over again.

Chapter 3

THE HERMIT

IT DID not take long for Romanus to discover that Benedict was really in earnest about being a hermit. Finally he agreed to take the boy to a cave and to give him a garment like his own—a rough tunic made of sheepskins.

"Since you're so new to the life, I'll come each day with a little food," he said kindly. "Otherwise you might starve to death in these hills."

Benedict smiled at such understanding. "You won't tell anyone about me, Romanus? You see, if Cyrilla tries to find . . ."

"I shall tell no one, young sir. On that you may depend. And if it's really God's Will that you serve Him here in the wilderness, you will do so. Never fear."

The boy sighed happily. "May you be blessed for those words, Romanus! And now—you'll take me to the cave?"

The man nodded. He had a strange feeling that this boy was no ordinary soul. Without a doubt there was some great work God intended him to do.

"Follow me," he said. "The cave lies over this way."

So it was that Benedict became a hermit. The

cave to which Romanus finally brought him was a
narrow ledge in the side of a hill. Far below, cutting
its way through a rocky gorge, rushed the river
Anio. There was no sound in this wilderness of
trees and rocks but the murmur of the river. And
the song of many birds. Truly, it was the very place
for a hermit.

As time passed Benedict grew strong and hardy.
His cave was open to the weather, but he learned
how to protect himself from rain and cold.
Romanus was faithful, too, coming regularly from
his monastery with food. All in all, the boy had no
regrets for having left the busy streets of Rome.
Had he not learned many things in his cave that he
would never have learned in school?

"Lord, keep on teaching me," he often prayed. "Let
me know more about You, so that I may love You
more. And show me how to pray well!"

Three years passed. Benedict was very happy in
his cave, never dreaming that soon God would give
him a new work to do. Yet God had other plans for
him. Although he had thought to hide himself from
the world, there were people in the hills who now
knew quite a bit about him. Simple peasants, they
had chanced upon his cave while out hunting
game. At first they had been a little frightened at
finding a strange young hermit in their hills, but
their worries soon disappeared. They found
Benedict kind and interested in their welfare. As
time passed, they sought him out more frequently.

"Why do you live like this?" they wanted to know.
"Who is this God you serve so faithfully?"

Benedict, who had sought to escape from the society of men, soon found himself acting as teacher and spiritual guide to the unlettered peasants. He told them stories of the saints. He explained the meaning of life and death, how a man's chief task in this world is to seek God and praise His goodness.

"This is wonderful," said one peasant. "Tell us more, good Brother."

So Benedict taught the peasants, and his fame spread rapidly throughout the hill country. Subiaco, the place where he lived, became a spot where gathered simple men who wanted to know about God. Regularly, they would clamber up the rocky side of the hill to hear him speak. Among other things they learned that their new friend had a twin sister at home, a girl named Scholastica. She had consecrated herself to God and someday would probably dedicate her life to His service.

"But your food, good Brother!" exclaimed one of his new friends one day. "How are you able to get enough to eat, if you spend all your time in prayer?"

Benedict smiled and told the peasants about Romanus. Almost every day the good monk came with a package of provisions. These he tied to a long rope which was let down over the side of the hill. A little bell was attached to the rope. When it rang, Benedict knew his daily meal was at hand. All he had to do was to take the package that dangled in front of his cave. Only once had the plan failed. That was the day the Devil had

HE EXPLAINED . . . HOW A MAN'S
CHIEF TASK IN THIS WORLD
IS TO SEEK GOD AND PRAISE HIS GOODNESS.

thrown a stone and broken the bell.

"The Evil One has little liking for those who try to seek God," said Benedict. "But should we be afraid of his tricks, my brothers? Ah, no! We should keep on with our prayers and good works. God is on our side. He will never desert us."

Faith

The peasants went away, filled with much admiration for their new friend. Repeatedly they told their wives and children about the hermit of Subiaco.

"Perhaps you should take him a little food once in a while," said the women. "If he is a young man from the city, he may not be strong enough to lead a hermit's life."

"He needs nothing from us," replied the husbands. "The good monk Romanus comes each day with all that is necessary."

Unfortunately Benedict had never told the peasants that there were a few times when Romanus was unable to make the long journey to his cave. After all, the good man was no longer young. To reach the spot where he could let down his rope was no small feat, with rocks and brambles everywhere. And he could not send another man in his place, for he had promised Benedict long ago never to tell of his whereabouts.

It was one Lent, when the hermit of Subiaco was about twenty years old, that the visits of Romanus ceased entirely. For the first few days Benedict managed to live on the herbs and wild berries that grew among the rocks, but after that he became quite weak. He said nothing to his friends, the peasants, however. After all, had not Christ fasted for forty days in the wilderness? Had not many great saints done the same? Why should he seek for comforts when presented with a good chance to suffer for his own sins and those of men and women living in the world?

"Lord, You won't forget me," he prayed. "If it's Your Will that I stay here on earth to give You glory, You'll see that I have everything I need."

Faith and Hope, two virtues belonging to all great souls, was not lacking in Benedict. One morning he heard a noise in the wild growth surrounding his cave. Twigs were crackling underfoot. Small rocks were being dislodged. Someone, a peasant, no doubt, was at hand.

But the stranger was no peasant. He was a priest. The previous night he had heard a heavenly voice bid him search the hills near Subiaco for a hermit in need of food. Now he had come, through miles of wild country, with a basket of provisions on his arm.

"Peace be with you, Father," said Benedict gratefully. "This cave is but a poor place, yet it may serve you as a shelter. Will you come in and rest?"

The priest looked at the gaunt young man before him. Never had he seen such courteous manners, nor such kindness as shone in the dark eyes which sought his own. Truly, this must be the holy hermit he had been told to help.

"My son, I have come to celebrate with you the Feast of Our Lord's Resurrection. Here are meat, bread, wine, fruit . . ."

Benedict smiled wanly. "Good Father, is it really Easter Day?"

"What other day, my son?"

"Then Lent is over!"

The priest nodded. It was only too clear that the hermit of Subiaco did not keep track of the days. Living in the wilderness, with only the wild things of the hills for company, he had forgotten that in the world outside men clutched eagerly at the hours. With them they could make fortunes, win battles, enjoy the luxuries of life. To Benedict, time was merely something whereby he could continue giving himself to God in prayer and sacrifice.

The boy and the priest spent a pleasant day together. As the visitor arose to go, towards evening, he turned impulsively to his young companion.

"My son, I've a feeling that you won't be a hermit much longer."

"Not be a hermit!"

"No. I think you'll be a monk, bringing the truths of our Holy Faith to many men."

Benedict shook his head. "I have never wanted to live in a monastery."

"Sometimes, my son, the plans we cherish are not those which God has in mind for our salvation. Sometimes even a good man may be a little selfish."

Benedict was silent. Although it was hard to admit it even to himself, he had often been bothered by that very thought. This quiet life of a hermit with so few human worries: was it fair that he should know such peace while millions of his fellowmen struggled to earn a living in the world?

While young men died in battle? While children
went ignorant of the truths of religion?

"You agree with me, I think?"

Benedict smiled slightly. "I don't know, Father.
What I do know is that I've been happy here at
Subiaco. My Lord has taught me many things in
prayer. But if it should ever be His Will that I go
elsewhere . . ."

The priest smiled. "I shall pray for you, my son.
And you will do the same for me. May the Holy
Spirit guide us both!"

Chapter 4

A NEW WORK

IT WAS a few weeks later that other visitors came to Benedict's cave. The newcomers were monks whose monastery was at Vicovaro, some eighteen miles away. The young hermit received them kindly, wondering all the while what it was the strangers wished of him. He had not long to wait, however. Recently the monks had lost their Father Abbot through death. Of course they could elect one of their own number to the responsible post, but word of Benedict's holiness had reached their ears.

"You'll come and help us?" they asked the young hermit. "You'll be our Father Abbot?"

Benedict did not know what to do. In his heart he felt that his way of life and that of the monks would never agree. Yet suppose his visitor of Easter Sunday had been right? That God no longer wished him to be a hermit? Suppose it was in the monastery of Vicovaro that he could be most useful to his neighbor.

"I'm too young to be your leader," he said finally. "I know nothing of life in a monastery."

"But you're a man of prayer. That is the most

23

important thing. In God's Name, say you will come!"

There was no doubt that the monks were very much in earnest. Finally Benedict agreed to go with them—to be their Abbot, to teach them what he knew of spiritual things.

"May the Lord bless this venture," he thought. "It's hard for me to leave the cave where I have been so happy."

When Benedict arrived at his new home he found the surrounding countryside much like that of Subiaco. The river Anio was still in sight, coursing along a rocky bed on its way to join the Tiber. There were the usual miles of rock and forest, too—the wilderness which never yet had been subject to the plow. The real surprise came later, however, when the monks took their new Abbot on a tour of the monastery. This establishment, built into a rocky cliff, consisted of a series of caves—each six feet long, four feet wide and eight feet high. The entrance to these caves was through the top, by steps hewn out of the rock. Each cave had a small window that looked out upon the river. There was no furniture, only two ledges cut into the damp walls.

"It is here we try to serve God," the monks told Benedict. "See how poor everything is, how we have allowed ourselves no comforts!"

The new Abbot nodded. "And your rule of life? Tell me about that."

The monks stared at their young leader. They had never had a rule of life. Each had spent his time as he saw fit. There was no established hour for rising or going to bed. Even the amount and kind of prayer was a matter of personal choice. The chief merit of the life at Vicovaro was its poverty.

After Benedict had visited the chapel, a large grotto hewn out of the rocks on a lower level than the cells, his heart was increasingly troubled. How could these men hope to be saints when they did not practice the virtue of obedience? What was the real value of voluntary hardship when the soul was a stranger to humility?

"My brothers," he informed the monks presently, "we must have order in our lives. We must live as a family obedient to its father. I say there shall be a rule of life at Vicovaro, a rule to which each man shall be subject."

The monks listened silently. This indeed was a new idea and one filled with possible difficulties. Surely their young Abbot did not mean what he said!

But Benedict was very much in earnest about making a rule for the monastery. As the weeks passed and he found that some of his followers were not obeying his few simple rules, he rebuked them gently but in no uncertain terms.

"Remember Lucifer, my brothers? He was once a shining spirit, the most beautiful of all the angels. Then pride entered his heart. He would not serve. And the Lord cast him out of Heaven forever!"

Such words were not humbly received, however. Secretly the monks were beginning to criticize the youth who sought to tell them what it meant to be a saint. Who was he, anyway? Little more than a boy who had run away from school! A peculiar character, who had lived three years like a wild animal in the woods!

"We made a grave mistake in bringing him here," whispered one monk. "He would rule us as though we were children."

Benedict knew what was going on behind his back, and his heart ached. The few rules he had made were not too hard. He himself willingly kept them. But these monks were lazy. When the bell sounded for prayers, many did not bother to come to the chapel. They did not feel like praying, they said. They would pray tomorrow.

"Lord, what shall I do?" thought Benedict. "I don't want to be harsh. I only want to help these brothers know and love You more."

During these first unhappy weeks the youthful Abbot's thoughts often turned to his peaceful cave at Subiaco. What had happened to his friends the peasants? Who was instructing them in the Faith? Who was seeing that the newborn children of Subiaco were brought to church to receive the saving waters of Baptism?

Although Benedict knew that the monks were no longer his friends, he never guessed the bitterness of their feeling against him. The time was fast approaching, however, when matters were to come to a head. One day at dinner the server brought in and set down before Benedict a goblet of wine. In his customary fashion, the young Abbot raised his hand in blessing high over the vessel. To his amazement, the goblet suddenly broke in two. It was as

TO HIS AMAZEMENT THE STURDY GOBLET
SUDDENLY BROKE IN TWO.

though he had cast a stone, instead of a prayer, at the mealtime drink.

Benedict stared at the widening pool of liquid on the floor. There was no doubt about it. This wine had been no fit drink. Evil hands had poisoned it.

"My brothers," he said quietly, "may Almighty God have mercy upon you!"

In the large square room that had been hollowed out of the rock, where no sunlight ever penetrated, the monks squirmed. The plan to remove Benedict from their midst had failed. What would he do, now that he realized there had been a plot to take his life?

"It was just an accident," faltered one monk. "Believe us, Father Abbot. The goblet was old and cracked."

Benedict's face was stern. "Why have you treated me this way? Did I not tell you before that my ways and yours would never agree? Go then, and seek an Abbot according to your way of life, for me you may have no longer!"

There was silence as Benedict strode from the room. Looking at his stern face, the men responsible for the plot shivered. The Abbot was going to rouse the countryside against them. His friends the peasants would come with scythes and pitchforks to kill everyone at Vicovaro.

But this was not Benedict's plan. He wanted only to return to his cave at Subiaco. Here he would be a hermit once again, serving God in prayer and sacrifice.

Chapter 5

YOUTH COMES TO SUBIACO

IT DID not take long for the countryfolk at Subiaco to learn of Benedict's return. As the weeks passed, the path leading to his cave became again well-traveled. Once more the young hermit acted as teacher and guide. He told stories of saints, of holy men in far-off Egypt who had left the world so that they might become hermits in the desert and spend their days and nights seeking God. As before, the peasants at Subiaco were much impressed with these stories. In fact, some of them experienced a sudden and wonderful desire to seek God, too—to live as desert hermits in poverty and hardship. But how? They were ignorant and unlettered. They knew little about religion. And there was no desert near Subiaco.

"My friends," said Benedict one day, "I have spent many hours asking God to enlighten you and me. I think the answer has come at last. With His help we shall form a little colony here at Subiaco. But we shall not be hermits. We shall live together as monks, helping one another in prayer, in study, in work with our hands. In this way our little family can discover what is meant by peace."

The peasants of Subiaco were delighted. Within a short time twelve men came to Benedict. Humbly

they acknowledged obedience to him as to a father.
In return, the youth promised to guide and cherish
them as his own sons. Having spent several years
in school, first at Nursia, his birthplace, later at
Rome, he could at least teach his friends to read
and write. Then, with God's help, all would learn to
work with their hands. For even holy men must
eat, must provide against illness and future need.

"We shall clear the land," said Benedict. "We shall
plant crops. Ah, my brothers, the Devil always has
a hard time tempting busy men!"

So it was that the countryside at Subiaco soon
underwent considerable change. The fertile ground,
plowed and carefully cultivated, now produced sufficient food to supply the needs of Benedict and his
followers. There was even enough left over for the
use of the poor.

As time passed, word of what was taking place at
Subiaco spread far and wide. Other peasants came
to join the venture, to become members of
Benedict's family. Once entered upon the peaceful
life of prayer and work, few felt the urge to leave it.
The original number of twelve monks gradually
increased, so that it was necessary to erect many
more buildings. These were plain wooden shelters,
sufficient but to provide protection from the rain
and snow. Each housed twelve men, with a leader or
Abbot in command.

"Why didn't someone think of this before?" asked
a young monk one day. "Before I knew Father
Benedict, I scarcely had enough to keep alive. I was
ignorant of God and His Truth. If I had an ambi-

tion, it was to be stronger than my neighbor and wealthier, so that I need not be hungry or cold."

"And it's different now?" asked another.

The young monk smiled. "Very different," he said. "Father Benedict has shown me the value of prayer and work. Truly, they are powerful weapons, the only ones that can undo the harm caused by bloody swords."

The others nodded. Father Benedict had taught them many things, including the story of the suffering that wars had brought to their native land. Now they understood why so many people in Italy were poor and starving and uneducated. During the previous hundred years, powerful barbarians from neighboring lands had swept across the country and laid it waste. These men, ignorant of Christ's teachings, had gloried in personal ambition. They had sought to conquer huge tracts of land for their own use, caring little for the dignity of their fellow-man or the sacredness of his property.

"But it's different now," continued the young monk. "Once people have heard about Subiaco, how we have made the fields yield enough to support a hundred men, they'll begin to do the same. There won't be any more wars. Everyone will want to *pray and work*. Father Benedict calls this *Ora et labora*. Soon he will be the most famous man in the country!" Humility

Benedict, however, had no desire for fame. Now that Italy was enjoying a semblance of peace under the rule of Theodoric, King of the Ostrogoths, he wished only to serve others, to repair the

destruction caused by the plundering armies of
Alaric, Attila, Genseric, and the other barbarian
leaders. To this end he prayed, taught, and labored
with such zeal that presently the souls under his
care caught the fire of his spirit. Charity flour-
ished at Subiaco, and peace, so that the men who
had been but poor pagans, inclined to idolatry
and deceit, proved to be the stuff of which saints
are made.

As was only natural, fame did come to Benedict
with the passing years. Even in Rome he and his
work became the topic of conversation. Many
wealthy nobles journeyed out to Subiaco to see for
themselves what this remarkable monk was doing.
When they returned, it was with hearts filled with
admiration. The boy of Nursia who had run away
from a Roman school at the age of seventeen was
now directing a really wonderful school himself. He
was teaching unlettered peasants to be monks.

"But why?" asked certain people in Rome. "We
have many monasteries here. Why should Benedict
start another at Subiaco?"

Those who had visited Subiaco were quick to
reply that Benedict's monastery was no ordinary
one. He required his followers to till the soil, to
work with their hands at humble tasks. He
required them to foster charity in their hearts, and
obedience. The monks were divided into groups of
twelve, with an Abbot at the head of each group.
They lived in small wooden monasteries, of which
there were now twelve, built within a radius of two
miles from Subiaco. From his own little monastery,

dedicated to Saint Clement, Benedict watched over the welfare of the entire colony.

"I've never seen such peace," reported one visitor on his return to Rome. "A trip to Subiaco is worth a dozen sermons."

One day, in the year 522, the Abbot of Subiaco found himself confronted by two Roman noblemen, Equitius and Tertullus, each of whom led a young boy by the hand. As the little party approached, Equitius spoke:

"Father Benedict, we've brought you our sons. Their names are Maurus and Placid. Will you take them into your monastery?"

Benedict looked at the boys. Maurus was about twelve, Placid seven. Like their fathers, they were dressed in rich garments.

"They're good youngsters," Tertullus hastened to add, taking Benedict's silence for disapproval, "intelligent and well-trained. You won't have any trouble with them."

"They're healthy, too," added Equitius. "They could be quite useful in a country place like this."

The Abbot of Subiaco, now a man of forty-two, put his hands on the heads of the young strangers. "And what do you think, my sons?" he asked kindly. "Would you really like to be monks?"

Maurus, the older boy, nodded gravely. "Yes, Father Abbot. I'd like to be a monk. But not in Rome. I want to serve God here."

Little Placid nodded vigorously. "I want to serve God here, too," he declared in a fresh, clear voice. "I like Subiaco."

"FATHER BENEDICT,
WE'VE BROUGHT YOU OUR SONS."

The Abbot smiled. His original disciples had been far older than Maurus and Placid. Lately, however, wealthy Romans were becoming interested in the changes taking place at Subiaco. Repeatedly they asked that the monasteries beside the river Anio be opened to their younger sons and brothers so that the latter might have a truly Christian education. Already several boys had been received. Known as "Oblates," or "gifts to God," these youngsters followed the regular monastic routine. They learned to pray and work in the fashion of their elders. They also went to school. Later, when they were old enough, they would receive the habit of a monk.

"You'll accept these lads, Father Abbot?" asked Tertullus anxiously. "You'll train them to be good Christians?"

Equitius made a motion with his hand, and the boys withdrew a short distance. "Father Abbot," he whispered, "you see before you two men who would be monks themselves if circumstances were only favorable."

"What keeps you away, my friends?"

Equitius sighed. "We have many duties in the world, Father Abbot. We cannot leave our wives, our other children, our business affairs. But we can offer these boys to God in place of ourselves."

Tertullus nodded. "Our neighbors have done it, Father Abbot. They tell us your school at Subiaco is far better than any in Rome."

Benedict smiled as he gazed toward the prosperous fields and gardens, the scattered monasteries where even now dozens of men and boys were busily engaged in varied tasks. It was true. "The School of the Lord's Service," which had had its beginning twenty years ago in a poor hermit's cave, was now a thriving place.

"God is good to generous souls," said Benedict gently. "My friends, He will bless you in a wonderful way for giving Him these sons."

Chapter 6

A LATE NIGHT WALK

MAURUS and Placid were soon much at home at Subiaco. Their regular schooling continued as at Rome, but now there were many new things to learn. For the first time in their lives the two boys discovered the meaning of manual labor. They planted crops, they mingled with others who had been but peasants in the world. They learned to be useful in many little ways. Then, at stated hours, they followed their elders to the public oratory to offer praise to God.

At first this type of prayer, the group chanting of the Psalms, seemed a little strange. The words were always the same. Week in, week out, the one hundred and fifty Psalms were solemnly chanted by Benedict and his monks. Sometimes these ancient prayers were joyful, praising God for His goodness, His power. At other times they were sad, asking for help. They told of sorrow for past sins. They begged for mercy and forgiveness.

"There's no better way to pray than the one our Father Abbot has found," said Maurus one day. "He calls it 'the work of God.' Placid, we're lucky to be living at Subiaco. The Abbot is our father and we

his children. As a family we offer praise to God, not
only because we want Him to give us things but
because we know He deserves our praise. It's a lot
different out in the world, though. People are
unhappy because they have no one to teach them
important things like this. They're always trying to
get more money, more power. That's why there are
wars."

Placid nodded. "Father Benedict could change all
this," he declared firmly. "He knows how to make
people happy without any fighting."

It was true. Benedict continually preached the
gospel of peace. He insisted it could be found by
every earnest soul, through prayer and work. As a
result, everyone at Subiaco came to realize that the
Father Abbot was a very wise man. The boy Oblates
were particularly fond of the zealous monk. He
taught them to read and write, to raise crops, to
care for sheep and cattle. He saw that they had
enough to eat, proper clothes, sufficient rest. More
than that. He taught these younger disciples one
very important lesson: that there can be no lasting
happiness in this world unless man pays constant
honor to God. A person who serves God to the best
of his ability cannot hate his fellowman or envy his
possessions. All he can do is recognize in that fellowman his own brother, created to be another child
of God and possessing an immortal soul destined
for eternal happiness.

One day a little group of monks came to Benedict
with a problem. They wished to move their three
monasteries, which were a mile or so distant and

situated atop a mountain, to a more convenient place.

"It's too hard to get water from the lake, Father Abbot," explained the spokesman. "The path to the valley runs along the edge of a steep cliff. Every time we go for water we fear for our lives."

Benedict smiled. He well knew the path in question. "Is that all, my brothers?" he asked. "You only wish to move closer to the lake?"

The monks nodded. Theirs was a reasonable request. Doubtless the good Abbot would give them the required permission at once. But Benedict had other ideas. Dismissing the monks with a few kind words, he bade them not to worry or think of moving closer to the lake.

The monks went back to their mountain home a bit puzzled. This was not the treatment they had expected.

"Perhaps Father Abbot only wishes to test our obedience," said one of them, finally. "Certainly he has no desire that we slip from the path with our water pails and fall over the cliff"

The monks were right. The holy Abbot did not wish his followers any unnecessary hardship. Late that same night he awakened Placid and brought him, sleepy-eyed and astonished, to his cell.

"My son, you and I are going for a walk," he said.

A hundred questions were on the boy's tongue, but he held his peace. Already he had learned that no one questioned orders at Subiaco.

"I'm ready, Father Abbot," the lad announced cheerfully.

Benedict smiled and took his young disciple by the hand. In a short time the two had disappeared into the night.

The path chosen by the Abbot was the narrow and difficult one leading to the three mountain monasteries. Placid walked slowly and carefully behind his beloved friend. Where were they going at this hour of the night? Why was he abroad with the Abbot of Subiaco while all others slept? What was going to happen?

Far below, its waters silvered by a newly risen moon, the river Anio rushed through its narrow gorge. Placid stole a quick glance at the valley. He could make out the lake where Maurus and he were accustomed to fill their water pails each day. This lake had an interesting history. Centuries before, the Emperor Claudius had ordered barriers erected across the river. The result was a large and beautiful lake, suitable for water sports and bathing. Here the Emperor had come with his family and servants whenever he wished a change from the noise and heat of Rome. His splendid villa was no longer standing, but Placid knew the ruins were still there. He knew about a second lake, too—a mile or so distant—also the result of man-made barriers across the Anio. From this second lake the river dropped some twenty feet into its ancient bed. Later it joined the Tiber, close to Rome.

There was little time to spend in gazing at the valley, however. Placid had all he could do to follow the Abbot up the ever-steepening path. Only a few inches away loomed a dark and forbidding chasm.

But he dared not think of that. Or of the chill wind that whistled so strangely through the rocks. He could only hope that the night's adventure would turn out well.

Presently the dark outlines of three buildings came into view. Placid, now much out of breath, knew these were the monasteries where lived the monks who had complained that day about the difficulty of securing water. But there was no sign of the monks now. All was quiet and deserted.

As the boy reached the summit, he turned eagerly to his leader. What was going to happen now? Were the monks to be awakened? Were the monasteries to be moved to the valley in the middle of the night? How exciting!

But the Abbot did not share his young friend's eagerness. His face was pale. He seemed to be struggling with some great problem.

"Kneel down, my son," he whispered. "We're going to pray for the welfare of these sleeping brethren."

It seemed a long time to Placid that he and his Father Abbot knelt there, quiet and motionless, on the very summit of the mountain. The wind whined and moaned about them. The moon stole behind a cloud. Somehow it seemed as though they were the only two people remaining in a barren world. But the boy knew the Abbot had forgotten the bleak surroundings. His lips moved silently. From time to time he raised his arms to Heaven as though he would seek some great favor. Looking at him, a great wave of longing filled the youngster's heart.

"I WANT TO BE ABLE TO PRAY LIKE THIS."

"I want to be like the Father Abbot," he thought. "I want to be able to pray like this, too."

Presently Benedict bent over and fumbled with the rocky soil. Finding three loose stones, he placed them together on the spot where he had prayed. Then he rose to his feet. His face was not solemn now, but full of a strange joy.

"Come, my son," he said kindly. "God has been very good. He has heard our prayers."

Placid scrambled eagerly to his feet. "What do we do now, Father Abbot?"

Benedict smiled. "We go back to Subiaco in peace," he said.

Chapter 7

WONDERS BY THE WATER

THE next day excitement was at a high pitch. The monks from the three mountain monasteries had come again to the Abbot to ask permission to move closer to the lake. Once more their request had been refused and they had been told to return home. If they looked carefully on the summit of the mountain, Benedict said, they would find three stones placed together. A little digging would reveal an abundant spring.

"And that's just what's happened!" Placid declared excitedly, as he came upon Maurus gathering wild berries. "Our Father Benedict is a saint! Who else could make water flow from the dry ground? Oh, Maurus, aren't you glad we came here?"

The older boy nodded. Subiaco was the most wonderful place in the world. And there was no greater man than Abbot Benedict.

It was a few days later that Maurus was summoned to the Abbot's cell. As soon as he entered the room the boy sensed that something was wrong.

Benedict, usually so calm and serene, stood staring strangely out the window.

"You wanted me, Father Abbot?"

Benedict nodded. "Go at once to the lake," he commanded. "Our brother Placid is in danger of his life."

A hundred questions flashed through the boy's mind. Just a few minutes before, Placid had been sent to get some water. Had he lost his footing on the slippery bank and fallen into the lake? Was he in danger of being drowned? There was no time for questions, however. Obedience was the rule at Subiaco, an obedience prompt and humble.

"Placid's such a little fellow!" thought Maurus as he hurried from the Abbot's cell. "Dear Lord, don't let anything happen to him! Dear Father Benedict, pray hard!"

The twelve-year-old boy reached the lake just in time. Far out from shore, where he had been carried by the swift current, Placid was making a few last struggles for life. Heedless of his own safety, Maurus rushed to his young friend's aid and in a few minutes succeeded in bringing him to dry land. But when Placid, dripping and breathless, tried to explain what had happened, he found Maurus shaking with fright.

"I just walked on the water, Placid! In the name of God, how could I have reached you otherwise?"

"But it wasn't you who saved me!" cried the younger boy. "When I was struggling in the water I saw Father Abbot's cowl over my head. I reached up and took hold. That's why I didn't drown!"

Maurus stared in amazement. "But Father

PLACID WAS MAKING A FEW
LAST STRUGGLES FOR LIFE.

Abbot's in his cell! Look for yourself. Do you see him around here?"

Breathless and confused, the two boys hurried to find the Abbot. What had really happened? How was it that Maurus, unable to swim, had brought his young friend safely to shore? What was the meaning of Placid's words?

Concern vanished from the Abbot's face as the two boys presently stood before him. "Today both of you have learned the value of obedience," he said simply.

"*Obedience,* Father Abbot?"

"Yes. Maurus went at once to your rescue, Placid. He didn't stop to question me, to ask what the trouble was. Ah, my sons, obedience is a wonderful virtue! Without it one cannot enter the Kingdom of Heaven."

Maurus looked directly at the Abbot. "But it was you who did it all," he said respectfully. "As I was running to the lake I asked you to pray for both of us. Father Abbot, what should we have done without your prayers?"

Placid, now somewhat recovered from his harrowing experience, began to smile. "It wasn't Maurus who saved me, Father Abbot. It was you. Thank you so much for everything. Next time I go for water I'll try to be more careful."

The story of the recent wonder worked through the Abbot's prayers soon made the rounds at Subiaco. Over and over again Placid and Maurus were asked to describe it. Soon each of the boys became accustomed to relating his part in the recent miracle. Maurus had walked on the water. Placid had seen the Abbot's cowl over his head. Each owed his life to the prayers of the Abbot, those prayers which were so pleasing to God because they came from a heart burning with charity.

The story of Placid's rescue never ceased to be a source of wonder to the monks of Subiaco. To Brother John, once a pagan Goth, now a Christian and a devoted member of Benedict's family, it was the cause of special joy.

"The Father Abbot is a good man," Brother John told himself. "The Father Abbot is a wonderful man. Praise be to God for sending him to us!"

The words had a rhythm that pleased Brother John. He found it a pleasure to sing them out in a loud voice whenever he worked in the fields.

One morning the husky Goth was told to labor in a new location. He was to take his scythe and go down to the lake. There were some patches of ground there that needed clearing.

"You understand what to do, my son? asked Benedict.

Brother John nodded vigorously. "I'm to clear that land as it's never been cleared before, Father Abbot. And I'll do it, too. I'm no man for learning, but my muscle is good. Just feel it!"

The Father Abbot smiled. "God be with you," he said. "The land you clear today will give us food in a few months' time."

Presently Brother John was at the lake, the same body of water which had witnessed the

miracle of Placid's rescue. As he gazed at the
unruffled surface, joy surged in his simple heart.
What a good thing it was to be alive! To be strong
and healthy! To be a monk at Subiaco! Why, it was
enough to make a man sing for joy!

"The Father Abbot is a good man," Brother John
told the wild birds flying over his head. "The Father
Abbot is a wonderful man! God be praised for sending him to us!"

The blue waters of the lake rippled in the sunlight as the former barbarian, descendant of the
pagan armies that once had plundered Italy, sang
and worked with a right good will. Weeds and wild
growth flew recklessly as the scythe rose and fell
with clock-like precision. In an hour's time the task
he had been given was almost completed. There
remained but a small patch of underbrush a few
yards away.

"Weeds, weeds!" Brother John told himself happily. "What are they to me?"

Again the scythe began to flash in the sunlight.
Again song arose from the industrious monk as
from a mighty organ. But suddenly, as he gave a
furious swing, the steel blade of the scythe loosened
from its wooden handle. Like some strange silver
bird it sailed majestically through the air, then
dropped with a great splash into the lake.

"May Heaven help me!" cried Brother John.
"What have I done now?"

For a while the crestfallen monk stared in
silence at the lake, then at the useless wooden
handle before him. He wouldn't be able to finish

clearing the weeds now. More than that. Good tools were scarce at Subiaco. He ought to go at once and describe to someone the dreadful thing that had just happened.

"I guess I was careless," he told himself sadly. "And proud of my strength." And as he went in search of a monk to whom he might confess his fault, he thought of the Gospel read at Mass that very morning.

"Everyone who exalteth himself shall be humbled; and he who humbleth himself shall be exalted."

Brother John had gone but a short distance when he unexpectedly came upon Maurus, of late an assistant to the Abbot in the government of the twelve monasteries. At once he broke into hurried speech concerning the calamity which had just occurred.

"It was my own fault, Brother Maurus. I might have known that the scythe should have been treated carefully. But I was so anxious to do a good job, to make an impression on Father Abbot . . ."

The boy could not help smiling at the monk's distressed face, his awkward embarrassment. "Don't worry," he said kindly. "I'm on my way now to see Father Benedict. I'll tell him about your trouble and he'll make everything right."

"But he couldn't bring back the blade of steel to this wooden handle, Brother Maurus. It's at the bottom of the lake."

"He saved Placid from drowning. His prayers gave me the gift of walking upon the water."

The simple manner in which Maurus spoke

these words brought a glimmer of hope to the monk's eyes. "Maybe you're right," he said slowly. "God be praised, Brother Maurus! Maybe we'll see another miracle at Subiaco! Now what should I do while I'm waiting for you to return with Father Benedict?"

The boy laughed. "You could say some prayers yourself, Brother John. I'll be back in a little while, after I've talked to Father Benedict."

With childlike trust Brother John knelt down upon the rough ground, the wooden handle of the scythe clutched firmly in his hand. By the time Maurus had returned with the Abbot at his side, he had recited the Lord's Prayer at least a dozen times and had even made up some little prayers of his own. But he continued to kneel as the Abbot approached, his eyes upon the ground in confusion and misery.

"Father Abbot, while I was working at the lake I took pleasure in my great strength. I told myself there is no one at Subiaco who can clear land as well as I. Then I gave a great swing with the scythe, never thinking about its value . . ."

Benedict smiled. "There, there, my son. I know the story. Rise to your feet and don't worry any more."

"But the steel head flew off, Father Abbot! It's in the lake now!"

Benedict nodded and reached for the wooden handle Brother John still clutched in his hands. "Come with me," he said gently. "God is always good to those who trust Him."

The little party made its way to the spot where

Brother John had been working with such good will. For a moment Benedict stared at the lake in silence. Then, dipping the wooden handle into the water, he offered a short prayer. Maurus and Brother John watched anxiously. What was going to happen? Was there to be another miracle? Suddenly both cried out in amazement. A few yards away, the steel head of the scythe was bobbing merrily on the surface.

"May God have mercy on us!" cried Brother John, and fell to his knees a second time. "This is too much!"

Maurus, too, knelt down and watched in amazement as the piece of steel floated directly toward the bank. Presently the Abbot reached out the wooden handle. As though forced by some mysterious power, the gleaming steel attached itself to the wood. Quietly Benedict drew the rescued tool to land, then presented it to his bewildered follower.

"There, my son," he said gently. "Work on and be sad no longer."

Chapter 8

THE ENEMY STRIKES

THE occurrence of still another miracle at Subiaco brought additional fame to Benedict. Hardly a week passed that Roman noblemen did not journey out from the city to enroll their young sons in his school. Many others also came to offer themselves as monks. As the years passed, the Abbot no longer found it necessary to recruit his followers from among the rough dwellers in the hills. His name was on everyone's lips, and the colony beside the Anio now numbered many men from the upper classes in Rome. Prominent among these were two learned brothers—Speciosus and Gregory. They possessed a good education and were of great value as teachers and helpers.

"The Abbot of these monks is a real saint," one person told another. "Never has there been such a man who spent all his days in showing others how to live at peace with God, with themselves and with their neighbors."

"He preaches the nobility of toil, something we have not heard before," said another. "Because of his holy labors Subiaco has become the garden spot of Italy."

But there was one person who envied Benedict, whose heart filled with rage whenever wealthy Romans came to pay him homage. This was the priest Florentius, an Arian heretic, who lived in the neighborhood of Subiaco.

"Benedict's no saint," Florentius often told himself. "And he doesn't really work miracles. He just fools people in his clever way so that they think he's a great man and bring him money. Ah, me! Why don't they use their eyes? Why don't they realize I deserve some help, too?"

The travelers to Subiaco paid little attention to Florentius, however. Benedict was the man with whom they wished to speak. Benedict was the man who had started a new type of educational training for the youth of Italy. And Benedict was the man whose prayers were so powerful before the throne of God that nothing seemed impossible.

By the year 527, when the Abbot had been at Subiaco close to thirty years, Florentius could stand the painful situation no longer. He determined to send Benedict a little loaf of bread in which poison had been placed. In this way he soon would be rid of his unwelcome neighbor.

For friends to send one another small loaves of bread was a custom peculiar to Benedict's time. These gifts were known as *eulogia* and were meant to be affectionate reminders of the union existing between all Christians because of the Bread that is the Body of Christ. *Eulogia* were sent at all seasons of the year, and Florentius congratulated himself on the fact that no one would suspect him of a crime merely because he had tried to show his regard for the Abbot.

"It's a wonderful idea," he told himself confidently, "and one that can't go wrong. Benedict will eat the poisoned bread and be dead in a few hours. After that, maybe people will start to pay a little attention to me."

Poor Florentius! He once had been a good man, but long ago jealousy had filled his heart with an evil cunning. Now there was nothing he would not do to rid himself of what he considered unfair competition. After all, hadn't he lived at Subiaco longer than Benedict? Wasn't he a priest and the Abbot but a simple soul who once had been a hermit? It wasn't fair that important Romans should pay this nobody so much honor.

When Florentius' gift arrived with many extravagant words of praise, Benedict was divinely enlightened as to the true state of affairs. It was to be the story of Vicovaro and the poisoned wine all over again. Once more an enemy was striving to slay the peace he loved so well—the peace he had tried so hard to teach his monks.

"This bread is poisoned," Benedict told himself, gazing sadly at the little loaf Florentius had just sent. "Dear Lord, what do You want me to do?"

The problem was a serious one. There was not the least doubt about that. Benedict would naturally pray for his enemy, as he had done in the past, but what about future relations with Florentius? In a short while the misguided priest would know that his scheme had failed. Then what would happen?

What other dreadful plot would come into his head to harm the Abbot of Subiaco?

As Benedict sat in his cell, puzzled and unhappy, a raven which he had tamed some years ago flew onto the window ledge. The bird had come, as was its custom, for its regular noonday meal. Now it regarded the Abbot with a beady and expectant eye. "Where's my corn?" it seemed to say.

A little of the sorrow faded from Benedict's heart as he arose to greet his feathered friend. "Little brother," he said, pointing to the poisoned loaf, "take this bread, in the Name of Jesus Christ, and drop it in a place where it can harm no one."

The raven uttered a harsh croak and flew eagerly toward the loaf But presently it changed its mind, and repeated commands on Benedict's part could not persuade it to take the evil loaf in its beak and depart.

Benedict smiled sadly. "Even you know this bread is poisoned, little brother. But don't be afraid. It won't hurt you."

The raven continued to regard the loaf with a suspicious eye, fluttering and croaking as though in protest at the command the Abbot had given. Finally, after more coaxing from Benedict, and the promise that the usual meal would be forthcoming as soon as the task was done, the raven opened wide its beak, seized the evil loaf and with a mighty flap of its glossy wings departed with the unusual burden. When three hours had passed, it reappeared on the window ledge to receive the promised meal.

One thought was foremost in Benedict's mind as

THE RAVEN CONTINUED TO REGARD
THE LOAF WITH A SUSPICIOUS EYE.

he gave the bird a generous portion of dried corn. What would Florentius do next? In his blind jealousy he probably would stop at nothing.

Things were not long in happening. Furious at the failure of his first plan, Florentius decided to sow seeds of discord among the men who up until now had been Benedict's devoted followers. He put temptations in the path of the boy Oblates. He spread cunning lies. He did everything possible to make the monks of Subiaco feel they had made a mistake in pledging life-long obedience to the Abbot.

"What do you get out of it?" he inquired with mock sympathy. "You have to work like peasants. You have only the necessities of life. Dear brothers, how my heart aches for you!"

Benedict shuddered at such malice. Finally he decided there was only one thing to do. He could not bear to see his followers tempted to return to the world. To protect their God-given vocations he would go away from Subiaco. Maurus, now seventeen years of age, could be Abbot in his place. He was an able lad, strong and holy and wise. There was little likelihood that Florentius would trouble him.

"I'm the only one he hates," thought Benedict sadly. "Dear Lord, I'm sure this is the best way out of the difficulty."

There was great consternation among the monks of Subiaco when they learned that Benedict was going away. In vain his older followers tried to persuade him to stay, to fight Florentius and his wicked lies. Benedict refused. He had no use for fighting. During the thirty years he had lived at

Subiaco, first as a hermit, later as Abbot, he had preached the goodness and beauty of peace. He had taught men to throw away their swords and cultivate the peaceful arts. He had given his monastic family a special motto: *Turn away from evil and do good. Seek after peace and pursue it.* Why should he forget his own words now?

The day Benedict left Subiaco, headed southward in the direction of Capua, Florentius was beside himself with joy. Success was his at last. Never again would he have to see the Abbot honored by people of all classes. As he climbed to the balcony of his house, the better to observe the departure of his enemy, he noted that a little body of monks was accompanying the Abbot. Among them was the boy Placid, now twelve years of age.

"And where do they think they're going?" he muttered hatefully. "Don't they know Benedict's defeated forever? That they can't possibly have any happiness with him?"

As he stood there, rejoicing over Benedict's departure, Florentius noticed a peculiar creaking in the timbers supporting the balcony. Suddenly, the entire structure beneath him began to crumble.

"Help!" cried Florentius, realizing his danger. But the sound was muffled by the roar of falling masonry and the splitting of wooden timbers. A few minutes later a passing peasant discovered the accident and the lifeless body of the wicked priest. At once he ran to report the news to Maurus, recently appointed Abbot of the twelve monasteries.

"He's dead!" stammered the peasant, torn

between fear and a happy sense of relief. "He was crushed beneath a great beam!"

Maurus could scarcely believe his ears and at once sent a party of monks to investigate. When they reported that the peasant was right, that Florentius had perished miserably in his sins, Maurus made a quick decision. He would go after Benedict and persuade him that now there was no need to leave Subiaco. The man who had made such trouble was dead.

By hurrying as fast as they could, Maurus and a few companions finally overtook the Abbot. But the latter showed little joy over the news brought to him. Instead he ordered his followers to kneel by the roadside and offer some prayers for Florentius' soul.

"My brothers, how can we rejoice over another's misfortune?" he asked sadly. His eyes were on Maurus as he spoke these words, and the young man bowed his head in shame. It was true he had been happy about Florentius' death. In the excitement he had forgotten the great charity in the Abbot's heart, a charity that had never been denied to anyone, not even to an enemy.

"But you'll come back, Father Abbot?" he asked presently, feeling himself forgiven. "You will be our leader again?"

Young Placid looked hopefully at the Abbot, as did the other monks. No one felt like continuing the journey now. But Benedict shook his head.

"It is the Will of God that I leave," he said quietly. "Brother Maurus, return now to your duties at Subiaco. And may Heaven bless you in your new work."

Chapter 9

MAN OF THE MOUNTAIN

MANY thoughts were in Benedict's mind as he and his companions journeyed down the dusty road, the ancient Latin Way which led from Rome to Capua. The Abbot, now forty-seven years of age, was really not eager to leave Subiaco. Well he knew that wherever he settled he would have to repeat much of his former labor. Yet something told him he was meant to make this journey, to do what he could to spread the peace of Christ in still another part of Italy.

Sometimes he smiled a little as he and his companions plodded steadily southward and he realized the eagerness of the monks to know his plans. Placid in particular showed all the excitement of youth. He asked no questions, yet curiosity sparkled in his eyes.

"But what can I tell the lad?" thought the Abbot. "I'm as ignorant of God's plans as anyone."

It was a few days later that the little group reached the town of Casinum, halfway between Rome and Naples, and not far from the Liris river. In the days when the Caesars had ruled at Rome, Casinum had been a thriving center, but the barbarian invasions had changed everything. People had been too busy fighting wars to think of

tilling the fields or educating their children. Now
Casinum was little more than a struggling village.
The people were poor and ignorant. They worshiped pagan gods in the wooded hills above the
town, and there was no one who understood the
truths of the Christian Faith.

"I think we'll stop here," said Benedict suddenly.
"And for a little while, my sons, I shall leave you.
But I'll be back. Never fear."

The monks were sad at this unexpected news, but
when Benedict explained that he wished to spend
some days in prayer, so that God might enlighten
his mind as to their next move, they began to
understand. Long ago the Abbot had taught them
the value of never entering upon a piece of work
without first asking God's help.

"I'll be a hermit once again," he told them with a
little smile. "It's been a long time since I lived
alone."

During the days that Benedict lived as a hermit
on the wooded mountain overlooking the town, the
people of Casinum became much interested in
Placid and his companions. Who were they? Why
did they wear those coarse garments? And who was
this strange God they worshiped?

"He's the Creator of the world," said Placid briefly. "He's prepared a wonderful place called Heaven
for all who serve Him faithfully."

The people of Casinum ventured a few other
questions, too. Was the God of the monks greater
than Jupiter? than Apollo?

"There is none greater than our God," said

Placid's companions. "In a little while our Father Benedict will tell you about Him."

The people were amazed when they heard that the leader of the monks was even then living on the mountain that shadowed the town. A few made their way up the great height, which once had served as a Roman fortress, but they could find no trace of Benedict. He had disappeared into the thick woods. He was nowhere near the grassy clearings where the people of Casinum had erected shrines to Jupiter, Apollo and Venus.

"He's praying for you and for us," Placid explained. "He's asking our God to make known His Will."

An old man tottered toward the youthful speaker. "You're but a boy," he said wonderingly. "How is it you travel with these monks?"

Placid smiled. "I'm an Oblate," he explained. "Five years ago my father brought me to the Abbot as an offering to God."

The old man shaded his weak eyes. "I don't understand," he muttered. "An offering to God is a sacrifice. We offer the gods our finest animals. We do not offer children."

An older monk stepped forward. "Your offerings are soon burned to ashes, my friends, but the offerings of Christians continue to be pleasing to God because they are united to the merits of Jesus Christ."

There was a low murmur of astonishment at these words and the men and women of Casinum crowded still closer about the strangers. All eyes were on Placid and his companions, and every face wore a puzzled expression. It was clear that no one understood the words the monk had just spoken. But there was no unfriendliness. The people were eager to learn more of the strange Christian religion. They also wanted to meet the leader of these monks. From all accounts the Abbot Benedict was a great man. Even now he was going through a period of prayer and hardship so that his purified soul might more easily receive God's message.

Benedict remained in seclusion for several weeks, then returned to his followers with the news that they would stay where they were. Monte Cassino, the great mountain that reared above the town, was owned by Placid's father, Tertullus. It was Benedict's choice for the location of his new home. There was no doubt that very soon Tertullus would give permission for the necessary building.

"A mountain top's the best place for a monastery," Benedict explained. "One finds few worldly distractions in such a spot."

Placid was overjoyed at the news. He had known Monte Cassino belonged to his father, as well as other great tracts of land in Italy and Sicily, but never had he breathed a word of this to the other monks. If they already knew his father was a wealthy Roman noble, well and good. But on the trip to Casinum he had no wish to set himself up as a member of a wealthy family. Something told him this was not the thing to do, since some of his companions had been but poor peasants out in the world. The education they now possessed, the various skills, were entirely due to the Abbot's patient training.

As time passed, Benedict and his followers built their monastery on the very summit of Monte Cassino. They cleared the land as they had done at Subiaco, and laid out fields for their crops. A gently winding road was also constructed so that the people of Casinum and those from the nearby city of Capua might visit the lofty monastery without too much trouble.

Benedict's monks wore a very simple habit. It was patterned after the garb of the Roman soldier. The latter wore over his armor a woolen tunic that reached to the knees. The monk wore a woolen tunic also, but it was longer, reaching to the ankles. The soldier wore an apron for heavy work, with a hood to keep off the rain. The monk was provided with a loose flowing scapular and a cowl for head covering. Each wore a belt buckled about the waist. As for the boy Oblates, they simply wore the tunic and belt.

Little by little the local pagans became accustomed to the sight of their new neighbors and several were won over to the Christian Faith. They helped the Abbot clear the mountain of the many pagan shrines that were scattered throughout the woods. After he had purified the former temple of Apollo, they helped him erect there a chapel dedicated to Saint Martin of Tours. Where once had stood Apollo's altar, they helped build another chapel, this one dedicated to Saint John the Baptist.

Chapter 10

TRICKS OF THE DEVIL

IT WAS the story of Subiaco all over again. Prayer and work were bringing about an enormous change in the wild countryside. As time passed, even more people asked for the saving waters of Baptism. It seemed they could not stay away from the kind-hearted monk who taught the gospel of peace.

The Devil was not pleased at this turn of events, however. He, the father of jealousy and pride, did not like to see a good man successful.

"I'll fix things," he told himself. "I'll cause so much trouble on this mountain that no one will want anything to do with the Abbot. They'll think he's been cursed."

The Devil used every means in his power to accomplish this end. He appeared to the Abbot under various horrible forms. Sometimes it was as a fierce black dog, his sharp teeth gleaming with blood, his yellow eyes flashing fire. Again he would hide himself in a cloud of evil-smelling smoke, screaming and cursing and promising all manner of harm to those who helped the Abbot clear the mountain. No one but Benedict ever saw these visions, but everyone could hear the voice of the Evil One.

"In the beginning he calls Father Abbot by his first name," one monk told another. "Then, when the good man doesn't answer, he tries another method."

"I know," replied the second monk. "With my own ears I've heard him. He grows angry when Father Benedict pays him so little heed. Then he shouts: 'Maledict, Maledict, what do you want with me? Why do you persecute me?' Of course we both know what 'Maledict' means." The first monk nodded. "It means 'Cursed.' Only Father Benedict is anything but that."

It was soon evident that Monte Cassino once had been the scene of Devil worship. On the ground where Benedict and his monks were now raising a house of prayer, Lucifer had been honored and worshiped. Probably all this had taken place hundreds of years ago, even before it became popular in Italy to offer homage to Jupiter, Apollo and Venus.

"Now the Evil One doesn't want to give way to God," thought the Abbot. "He thinks he can frighten us into leaving this place."

But Benedict knew he would never depart from Monte Cassino merely because the Devil wished it. True, he had left Subiaco when trouble came, but it had not been through fear. It had been because he thought his presence was aggravating Florentius to wicked deeds. Not for any other reason.

Gradually Benedict's followers lost their fear of the Devil's screams and curses and of the hardships he loved to cause them. They realized the Abbot was

equal to every emergency and that his prayers
could send the Devil flying.

One morning the monks tried in vain to lift a certain stone that would be of use in building the new
monastery. They could not make it budge. Four men
pulled and tugged; then eight men, twelve men. The
stone seemed part of the mountain itself. Finally
the monks sent word to the Abbot that they needed
help. When the latter came to see what the trouble
was, he made the Sign of the Cross over the obsti-
nate rock. At once the stone could be lifted by one
man, as though it had no weight at all.

"The Devil was sitting on that rock," the monks
told one another earnestly. "But what can he do
against the Sign of the Cross? or the prayers of our
Father Abbot? Nothing at all!"

Benedict was just leaving his followers, after this
incident of the stone, when one of the monks cried
out in alarm. Enormous flames were shooting into
the air. The monastery kitchen was on fire!

"Father Abbot! What'll we do? We haven't enough
water to put out the flames!"

Benedict gazed toward the burning building.
"Make the Sign of the Cross on your eyes, my brothers. Then look at the kitchen."

Hurriedly the monks did as they were told, only
to discover that the huge blaze had disappeared.
"It's the Devil again," said Benedict quietly. "He
likes to make things hard for us."

Later, at a command from the Abbot, one of the
monks entered the kitchen. He came back with the
news that a bronze idol, discovered only recently

under the heavy stone, had been carelessly thrown
into a corner. It had not been broken into bits, as
Benedict had ordered, but was still in one piece.
Silently the Abbot strode into the kitchen with a
hammer and broke the idol into a thousand pieces.
Then he returned to his monks.

"I think everything is all right now," he said
quietly. "Don't be afraid, my brothers. There
won't be any more Devil's tricks for a while. Be of
good heart and continue your labors."

Benedict was right. For a few days there was
peace at Monte Cassino and the monks made good
progress on their new monastery. It was not a plain
wooden shelter this time. It was of stone, a material
that was very plentiful on the mountain top. But
one morning as the monks were busy erecting a
wall, the stones they had put in place began to
loosen. Presently, amid shrieks and cries, the whole
wall collapsed. When the dust had settled, it was
discovered that a boy Oblate had been buried in the
ruins. He was Severus, the son of a Roman senator.
The falling stones had crushed him to death.

As gently as they could, the frightened monks
examined the shattered young body. Was this
another trick of the Devil? Was it an illusion, as the
fire in the kitchen had been? Quickly the monks
agreed that it was not. Severus really was dead. His
body was bruised and his bones were crushed.

"Don't give up hope!" cried a monk suddenly.
"Let's take the lad to Father Abbot. His prayers
have worked miracles before."

So the little procession set out, the monks carry-

THE MONKS CARRYING THE LIFELESS BODY
ON A BLANKET BETWEEN THEM.

ing the lifeless body on a blanket between them. In a short time the whole dreadful story was being related to Benedict, who grew pale as he looked at the quiet young figure before him, covered with dust and blood.

"It's the Devil again," he murmured sorrowfully. "Ah, my brothers, how he hates us!"

The monks were silent. Severus had been only a boy. And he had been a good worker, quick and nimble with his hands. What a pity this dreadful accident had happened!

Presently the Abbot made a sign for the monks to leave. "Go back to your work," he said quietly. "And please pray for me."

When he was once more alone, Benedict knelt down beside the twisted body of his younger follower. Tears sprang into his eyes. He thought of the days when he, too, had been a teen-age boy, when he had fled from a Roman school to be a hermit.

"I had good health," he murmured. "God was ever generous to me. No dreadful accident ever struck me down."

Presently he began to pray, slowly and fervently, as was his custom. He begged God, through the merits of Christ's sufferings and death, to have pity on him and hear his request. He begged that life might return to the boy now cold in death.

"Severus was given into my keeping," he murmured. "Now harm has come to him because he did my bidding. Father in Heaven, have mercy on another father! Let Your power shine forth on this mountain so that all men may hasten to pay You homage!"

When three-quarters of an hour had passed, the monks laboring on the fallen wall looked up to see the Abbot coming slowly toward them. At his side walked a familiar figure.

"God be praised!" cried one monk, scarcely believing his eyes. "It's Severus!"

A thrill passed through the little group. It was Severus, the blood and dust removed from his face and clothes. And he was in perfect health! He didn't even walk with a limp!

As the two came to a stop, a few yards distant, the monks heard Benedict give the boy a brief command.

"Help rebuild that wall, my son. The Devil played another of his tricks a while ago and ruined all our labors."

The boy nodded and ran eagerly to take his accustomed place. Apparently he had not the slightest notion of what had happened less than an hour ago. If his eyes were a bit puzzled, it was for quite another reason.

"Why have I been out walking with the Father Abbot?" he was asking himself. *"Why haven't I been working on this wall with the others?"*

Chapter 11

THE WAY OF PEACE

BENEDICT had settled on Monte Cassino in the year 527. At about the same time Justinian became head of the eastern half of the Roman Empire, with headquarters at Constantinople. During the first few years of his reign, Justinian was very busy waging war against King Chosroes the First of Persia. When peace was declared in 533, the Emperor turned his thoughts to still other conquests. Wishing to claim the western half of the Roman Empire, he sent a fleet of five hundred transports, guarded by ninety-two war galleys, to north Africa. Two years later his able general, Belisarius, reported that a large part of Africa, formerly controlled by the Vandals, and before that by Rome, could be considered part of the Empire once again.

"And what now, sire?" asked Belisarius. "Do we go to Italy?"

Justinian agreed. Not only did he wish to govern the eastern Roman Empire, with headquarters in Constantinople. He wanted to govern the western Roman Empire, too, with headquarters at Rome. He wanted to be undisputed head of the entire vast territory. No man had held such an important position since the death of Emperor Theodosius the First, in 395. But it could be done, thought Justinian, through clever management and able armies. Theodoric, King of the Ostrogoths and former ruler of Italy, was now dead. And he had left no follower capable of succeeding to the throne. It was the very time for a strong man to strike.

Benedict heard with sorrow of Justinian's decision. He had never had any use for war. To him, happiness could be attained only through prayer and work, not through the brute force of armies or the pitiful glitter of gold. In the year 535, when the Emperor's victorious legions crossed from north Africa to invade Italy, the Abbot and his monks offered ceaseless prayer that God would avert the approaching catastrophe.

"It's the ordinary people who will suffer most," Benedict told himself. "The plain little families that don't ask for more in life than the chance to make a decent wage and raise their children in peace."

As though from a watch tower, Benedict observed the darkening scene from his monastery on Monte Cassino. His heart was sad at the thought of approaching hardships. War was such a complicated matter. Generally there was a mixture of right and wrong on both sides. In the present case Justinian was setting himself up as a liberator. He wanted to restore Italy to the Italians. He wanted to drive out the barbarian Ostrogoths, who knew nothing of literature, culture or the arts, and bring back the glory and the greatness of the Roman past.

But the Ostrogoths insisted on remaining where they were. They claimed they had won a rightful place in Italy over forty years ago when their king, Theodoric, had defeated the barbarian Odoacer. They saw no reason now why they should return to their own country in northern Europe.

"Things will go from bad to worse if we have war," thought Benedict. "Young men will be killed by the thousands. Taxes will rise. Farms will be neglected. Food will be scarce. Everyone will be dreadfully unhappy!"

But he did not take sides either with Justinian or the Ostrogoths. He remained quietly in his monastery on Monte Cassino. Here he guided his monks in the way of peace, as he had always done, and instructed the large number of boy Oblates brought to him for education. By now he was also busy with a piece of writing. This was the Rule by which he governed his monastery, the Rule that was destined to be famous throughout all Europe by the year 800.

This Rule was a complete and thorough one, setting forth what was expected of a monk living in Benedict's monastery. It explained how he was to study, to work, to eat, to sleep. Above all, it showed that a monk's chief duty was the praise of God. No day was to pass without his going several times to the oratory, in company with his brother monks, to offer group prayer to God in the chanting of the Psalms. This type of prayer fostered love, said the Abbot. It left no room for personal pride or ambition. It stressed the family spirit. There was nothing that should be preferred to it.

One day Benedict's followers came to him with some news. They were not the only ones on Monte Cassino who had dedicated themselves to lives of prayer. Not far away from the monastery lived a hermit. His name was Martin, and he was so eager to remain faithful to his difficult vocation that he had chained his foot to a large rock. In sun, rain and snow he never moved from his narrow cave.

"He leads a very hard life," said one monk in an awed voice. "He must be a saint, Father Abbot."

Benedict smiled. He had spent much time in reading about hermit life—in Egypt, Syria, Asia Minor, Greece and other countries of the east. He knew that in the third and fourth centuries thousands of men had sought to renew their spiritual lives by leaving the cities and going forth into the desert to discover the peace of Christ. There had been many holy souls among these hermits. Saint Paul the First Hermit, for instance, whose life Saint Jerome had written. Other men, Pelagius the Deacon and John the Subdeacon, had copied down the wise sayings of other dwellers in the desert. The life of the hermit St. Anthony had been written by Saint Athanasius.

Yet Benedict was inclined to be a little suspicious of hermits. Having been one himself, having led a solitary life for three years, he understood how some men fled to the desert only to escape responsibilities, so they would not need to be obedient to a superior. They told themselves they were very holy because of the hardships in their lives, while all the time their hearts were full of pride.

"Let's hope the hermit Martin is a saint," said Benedict kindly. "In the meantime, my sons, one of you may take him a message from me. Say to him these words: 'If you are a servant of God, let no chain of iron hold you, but the chain of Christ.'"

The monk who brought Benedict's message to the hermit Martin could hardly wait to see what the latter would do. Was he a proud man? Was he secretly puffed up because of the many sacrifices in his life? Would he be unwilling to break the chain that bound him to his cell?

There was not long to wait. When the gaunt old hermit learned that the Abbot of Monte Cassino had sent him a message, he received the monk kindly.

"What word do you bring?" he asked.

The monk cast a quick glance at the chain about the hermit's foot, the chain that proclaimed his holiness to the world. Then he repeated Benedict's words.

"If you are a servant of God, let no chain of iron hold you, but the chain of Christ."

The old hermit was overcome with surprise. It was a strange message to one who had undertaken a life of hardship so that he might save his own and other souls. But he uttered no complaint.

"Your Father Abbot is a saint," he said simply. "My brother, help me to do his bidding."

So the monk and the hermit, equipped with sharp stones, finally succeeded in breaking the iron chain. From now on Martin would be faithful to his hermit's vocation through love of God alone.

Benedict was delighted when he heard the news. To him, obedience was one of the great requirements for a happy life. When it was prompt and unquestioning, it showed that humility was strongly rooted in the soul. Then a person was well on his way to being a saint.

"We can learn a lesson from the hermit Martin," he told his followers. "He's a good man."

Chapter 12

BROTHER PETER AND THE LAMP

A LTHOUGH Benedict continually watched over the monks and Oblates, instructing them in the way of peace, sometimes he saw that all was not well in the monastery. Merely because a man had left the world to put on a monk's habit did not make him perfect. Benedict was particularly concerned over the case of Brother Peter. One night, as he was eating his supper, he called the latter to him.

"It's growing dark," he said. "Brother Peter, fetch a lamp and hold it for me while I eat."

"Yes, Father Abbot," replied the monk, and went to do as he had been told. But, as the minutes passed, Brother Peter grew impatient at being given such a simple task. He looked at the Father Abbot, quietly eating his meal. Then he looked at the lamp in his own hand.

"He's treating me as though I were a servant," he thought. "And I'm the son of a famous lawyer, too. Why couldn't he have asked someone else to hold this lamp? I should be doing more important things."

Benedict laid down his spoon. He knew what was

going on in Brother Peter's soul. The Devil was
tempting the young man to thoughts of pride. Long
ago he had stopped his other tricks—the setting of
fires, the knocking down of walls, the screaming
and cursing. Now he was taking other ways to upset
Benedict's work. He was sowing seeds of discontent
in men like Brother Peter.

The Abbot's face became stern. "Make the Sign of
the Cross on your heart," he ordered suddenly.

Brother Peter, a bit taken back, did as he was
told. But now hot anger flooded his cheeks. The
Abbot might be a holy man, but what right did he
have to speak so severely to the son of a famous
Roman lawyer? And how was it that he could read
a person's thoughts?

Suddenly Benedict rose to his feet. "Set down the
lamp," he said quickly. "Then call the brethren to
me. You are excused from further service."

Brother Peter, ashamed and humiliated, went in
search of the other monks. He was really angry,
especially when he saw the many figures hurrying
obediently to the Abbot's cell. In a short while
everyone would know the whole story.

"I wish I'd never come to this place," he muttered.
"What was so wrong in thinking as I did? I do
belong to a good family. And holding a lamp is a
task for a boy, not for me."

His pulses hammering with anger, Brother Peter
strode wildly through the corridors of the monastery. No one was in sight, most of the monks now
being with the Father Abbot. He was glad of this.
Glad, too, of the dim light in the corridor. It would

be quite a while before he felt himself again, able to face the others. Suddenly he caught sight of a familiar figure limping from the chapel. It was old Brother Luke, excused from his usual tasks because a few weeks ago he had tripped in the fields and hurt his leg.

"Good evening, Brother," said the latter happily. Then, noting the scowl on his friend's face, his tone changed. "What's the matter?" he asked anxiously. "Aren't you feeling well?"

Brother Peter tried to slip away with a few mumbled words, but Brother Luke was a persevering soul. "Tell me all about it," he coaxed. "You know Father Abbot has given everyone permission to amuse me while I'm laid up with this lame leg."

Brother Peter sighed. He didn't want to talk to anyone, certainly not to Brother Luke, one of the holiest of Benedict's followers.

"You'll know soon enough," he said abruptly. "So will everyone else."

A slight smile curved Brother Luke's lips. He reached out his hand to the younger man. "I'm a little tired," he said. "Maybe you'd help me to my cell?"

Presently, in some mysterious fashion, Brother Peter found himself blurting out the whole unfortunate story. The older man, as he settled himself on his hard bed, seemed a little amused at the jumbled narrative.

"Don't worry too much," he said gently. "The longer I live the better I realize that it takes the average man quite a while to get ready for Heaven."

"But you can't call having proud thoughts getting ready for Heaven! Or giving in to anger!"

The old monk was silent a moment. "Sit down," he said. "And don't be afraid you're breaking any rule, Brother. It's a real act of charity to keep a sick man company."

So Brother Peter sat down, on a small stool near the bed. A candle flickered fitfully on a nearby table, casting its shadow on the grey stone of the walls, the poverty of the little cell. The only furnishings were the bed, stool and table. And a large wooden cross over the door. Yet the place was not gloomy. The inner peace of the older monk seemed to lend an air of cheerfulness to the little room.

"I want to tell you a story," said Brother Luke suddenly. "It may make you feel better."

Brother Peter smiled wryly. "A sinner doesn't deserve any pampering. And that's what I am. A miserably proud man who has no place at Monte Cassino."

The older monk smiled. "We'll see about that later. Just now all you have to do is be quiet."

Brother Peter nodded. "All right," he said. "I'll listen to your story."

"Many years ago," began Brother Luke, "when our Father Abbot was governing his twelve monasteries at Subiaco, a young man came to him who wished to be a monk. Father Abbot received the stranger kindly. But after a few weeks had passed he saw that the newcomer was not much devoted to prayer. True, he went with the others to the oratory to chant the Psalms. He worked hard in

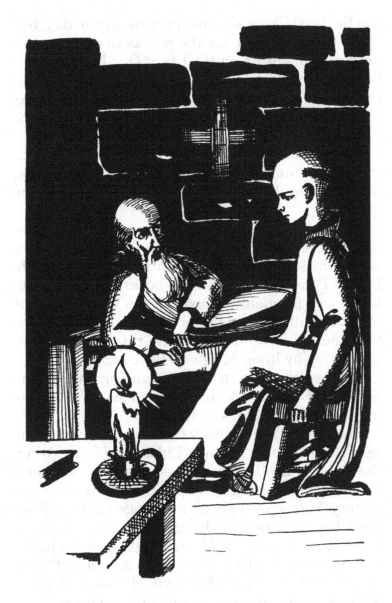

"JUST NOW ALL YOU HAVE TO DO IS BE QUIET."

the fields. He kept silence throughout the day. But when the time came for the monks to offer mental prayer, to meditate on the life of Our Lord and the heavenly mysteries, the young monk could not concentrate. He would slip quietly from his place, while all heads about him were bowed, and go for a walk."

Brother Peter looked up with interest. "What was the man's name?" he asked. But the older monk, carried away by his own words, did not hear the question.

"The Abbot Pompeianus, in charge of the monastery where the young monk lived, spoke to him many times of his fault," he continued. "He spoke to Father Benedict, too, and the latter did his best to sow a love for mental prayer in the newcomer. But to little avail. The monk managed to meditate with the others for two days. On the third, he went off wandering by himself, as was his custom."

Brother Peter was ready to inquire again as to the identity of the monk, but he had no chance. His friend was speaking once more.

"Finally Father Benedict said he would come again," continued Brother Luke. "This day, when the hour for meditation arrived, he went and knelt with the monks under Pompeianus' charge in their oratory. Very soon he saw a strange sight. A little black boy was standing beside the monk who could not stay at his prayers. He was tugging at his habit, and pointing to the open door. At once Father Benedict knew it was the Devil. He asked Brother Maurus, who had accompanied him to Pompeianus' monastery, if he could see the strange sight, too. Brother Maurus didn't see anything unusual. But when two days had passed, and Father Benedict and he had prayed very hard for the monk, Brother Maurus also saw the Devil, tugging at the monk's habit and urging him to leave the church."

Brother Peter bent forward eagerly. "What happened then?" he asked.

"Then? Why, a day or so later Father Benedict went after the monk. He found him wandering through the fields, quite content with himself, and pleased that he had escaped once more from the meditation he found so hard."

Brother Peter sighed. "I know that feeling," he said slowly. "There've been many times when I've found it almost impossible to pray."

"Father Benedict wasn't a man to be trifled with, however. He knew the Devil had obtained some strange hold over his young follower, that it was he who would not let the other stay at his prayers and thus give honor to God. So he picked up a stick and gave the young monk a hard blow."

"He hit him?"

"Yes. But the Devil was hurt more than the monk. From that day on he stopped bothering him at meditation. Never again was he able to lord it over the young man's mind."

Brother Peter was silent a moment, comparing the thoughts he had had but a few minutes before, while holding the lamp for the Abbot, with the thoughts entertained by the young monk who hadn't been able to stay at his prayers. There was no doubt about it. The Devil was very clever. From the beginning he had hated the way of peace which Benedict had laid down for his followers. He was still trying to destroy it, through pride and disobedience.

"As soon as I can, I'll tell Father Abbot I'm sorry for my proud thoughts," Brother Peter promised himself. "And I'll try not to grumble any more about being given small tasks."

Brother Luke raised himself on an elbow and coughed slightly. "You're not asleep, Brother?"

The younger man came back to himself with a start. "Oh, no!" he cried. "I was just thinking, Brother Luke."

"That's good."

"I was wondering about the monk in your story. Is he still living?"

Brother Luke nodded peacefully. "Oh, yes— through the mercy of God. Right now, though, he has a lame leg. Will you say a little prayer, Brother, that it gets better soon?"

Chapter 13

DISTANT HARVEST

BENEDICT loved his monks as a father loves his children. His one aim was to see them saints. Out of his own wisdom he instructed them in religious matters, teaching them how to chant God's praises in a becoming manner, how to sanctify their other tasks about the monastery. At stated intervals he told stories of great men who had sought and found God not so many years before. Saint Ambrose, Saint Augustine, Saint Jerome, Saint Cyprian, Saint Leo, Saint Basil—these names became well known to the monks and Oblates of Monte Cassino. They also learned of another holy soul, a man named Patrick. He had died in 493, about the time thirteen-year-old Benedict was leaving Nursia to take up higher studies in Rome. Patrick had been a missionary to the faraway country of Ireland. He had done wonderful things for the pagans dwelling there.

Not only the monks and Oblates heard these tales of the saints. Because Monte Cassino was so close to the well-traveled Latin Way, priests, Bishops and important laymen frequently came to hear the Abbot's instructions, too. One day, after

Benedict had given an especially inspiring talk, one of these visitors approached him with an unusual request. This man owned a large estate at Terracina, a town not far from Monte Cassino. He believed that if Benedict would send some monks to build a monastery there, much good would be accomplished. Pagans would be converted to the Christian faith, and wild country cleared and cultivated.

"It seems a good plan to me," the visitor told Benedict humbly. "I've been blessed with much wealth, Father Abbot. I'd like to provide for a monastery before I die."

The Abbot considered the idea carefully. Monte Cassino was now almost completed, with more than three hundred men and boys living within its walls. If it were really God's Will that a new monastery be founded, a few monks could easily be spared.

"I'll think about the matter," Benedict told the visitor kindly. "God bless you, my friend, for such a generous gift."

After praying earnestly for several days, Benedict was finally convinced that the monastery should be established. He chose twelve older monks, including the two learned brothers, Speciosus and Gregory, appointed an Abbot over them, then announced the news. The group was to leave Monte Cassino. It was to go to Terracina and begin the proposed monastery.

The monks did not complain, although their hearts were sad at leaving their beloved father. They were worried, too, about the building of the monastery. After all, what did they know of such a work?

Reading their thoughts, Benedict had pity on this first group of men to leave his care. "Don't worry," he told them kindly. "I'll come to you soon and show you where to build the oratory, the refectory, the guest house and all that is necessary. In the meantime, just trust in God. He is in your souls, as you know. Even when troubles come and He seems to have gone far away, He is still with you. Trust Him, my brothers."

faith

Time passed, and Benedict was very busy. Those close to him wondered when he would go to Terracina to fulfill his promise. But no one took the liberty to inquire, since such a matter was the Abbot's own business. As a result, there was much surprise when a visitor reported that the monks at Terracina were making good progress on the monastery Benedict had designed for them. Already the oratory was half completed.

"But Father Abbot never left here!" said the monks. "He couldn't possibly have designed this new monastery!"

Soon the whole story was out. Benedict hadn't left Monte Cassino, yet he had helped his children just the same. He had appeared to the Abbot and the Prior in a dream, instructing them as to the planning of their monastery. It was a new kind of miracle, people said, and a very convenient one.

Presently other wealthy men appeared on the scene with gifts of land for Benedict. One of these was Gordianus, a wealthy Roman nobleman. In the name of his wife, Sylvia, he presented the Abbot with a handsome villa near the town of Aquinum. Another benefactor was Tertullus, father of the monk Placid. Years ago he had given Monte Cassino into Benedict's keeping. Now he came forward with another valuable offering. It was the gift of eighteen farms in Sicily.

"Do as you please with this land, Father Abbot," Tertullus said. "I'd be happy, though, if you could send some monks to help convert the people. Sicily is full of barbarians."

Barbarians! This word was a familiar one to Benedict. His first monks had been these same unlettered men, rude dwellers in the hills of Subiaco. It was only later that things had changed and boys from the better classes in Rome, Naples and Capua had come to offer themselves to God in his monastery.

"Maybe I should send some of the brethren as missionaries," Benedict told himself. "The world is so hungry for God's peace."

Yet he did not speak these words aloud. He thanked Tertullus for his generous gift, then went to his cell to pray for guidance. As he knelt, he realized the truth of his good friend's words. Barbarians were very numerous in Italy and the islands of the Mediterranean. Even now the armies of Justinian were endeavoring to drive them back into northern Europe.

"It would be better to teach these poor people than to drive them away," Benedict thought. "Dear God, enlighten my mind! Let me know if some of my brethren should become missionaries!"

When a few days had passed, Benedict felt that God had made known His Will. The eighteen farms in Sicily represented a valuable piece of property. If Christian monks arrived to clear and cultivate it, they naturally would come in contact with their pagan neighbors. They would be called upon to explain their way of life, why they preferred to work at peaceful tasks while other men fought bloody battles. In the end there would be conversions, even as there had been at Subiaco and Casinum.

"I'll send a few monks to Sicily," thought Benedict. "And Brother Placid will be their leader."

Benedict had been deeply attached to Placid ever since the day his father had brought him, a boy of seven years, to the monasteries of Subiaco. He remembered the night when he had taken the lad to pray with him on the mountaintop. He remembered, too, when Maurus had saved the youngster from drowning. Somehow all these things might have happened only yesterday. But they had really happened long ago. Placid was no longer an Oblate, busy with little tasks suited to a child. Now he was twenty-one years old and a full-fledged monk.

"I'd better tell him the news," thought Benedict. "He'll be surprised."

Placid was more than surprised. For fourteen years he had occupied a humble position in Benedict's monastery. It was a little difficult to be suddenly placed in charge of several companions and ordered to undertake the building of a monastery. It meant responsibility on a large scale. It meant leaving Monte Cassino and the kindly Abbot who had taught him everything he knew. Yet Placid had been well trained in obedience and now he listened carefully to what Benedict had to say.

"Sicily's a wild place," continued the latter. "Your father tells me other men have seized his property from time to time and that it's in a bad state."

Placid nodded. "The land is near the coast, Father Abbot. Pirates often come there to plunder and destroy."

The Abbot was quiet for a moment. His eyes were fixed upon this serious young face before him, a face that showed no fear but only an eagerness to have a part in the distant harvest of souls.

Finally he spoke. "God bless you, Brother Placid. I've given you a hard task. But there'll be rewards, never fear. Rewards far past your dreams."

The young monk smiled. "I'll do my best to earn them," he said simply. "Please remember me in your prayers, Father Abbot."

It was a few weeks later that Placid and a dozen companions set out for Sicily. As the little band made its way down the mountain, Benedict raised his hand in a last fatherly blessing. Then a deep sadness settled over his soul. Placid was so young! The task before him so great!

"May the Lord protect him," he prayed silently. "He has a long and dangerous way to go."

Later that day, when he and his monks returned from working in the fields, Benedict went to his cell to write a letter. It was addressed to his

HIS EYES WERE FIXED UPON THIS
SERIOUS YOUNG FACE BEFORE HIM.

sister Scholastica. For some years the latter had
been living in the Monastery of Saint Mary at
Plumbariola, a town three miles away. Once a year
she and Benedict met, in a house halfway between
their respective monasteries. In a few days their
customary visit would take place. Yet the Abbot's
heart was too full of emotion to delay the news of
Placid's departure. In simple words he explained
what had just happened and begged his sister's
prayers and those of her community for the little
band of missionaries.

As he finished the letter, there was a knock at the
door. Benedict rose to open it and found his other
young disciple, Brother Maurus, waiting to see him.
During the years following Benedict's departure
from Subiaco, Maurus had acted as Abbot of the
twelve monasteries. Lately, however, he had come to
Monte Cassino to be the Abbot's assistant.

"Yes, my son?" said Benedict kindly, noting an
expression of concern on the younger man's face.
"Something's troubling you?"

Maurus nodded. "It's Agapitus, Father Abbot. He's
come again to get some cooking oil from Brother
Michael. But Brother Michael says we can't spare
any oil. We have only one small bottle left."

Benedict frowned. "Didn't I tell Brother Michael
two days ago to give the good man some oil, no
matter if we ran short ourselves?"

"Yes, Father Abbot. But Brother Michael says it's
foolish to be so generous."

Benedict looked at the letter he had just written
his sister. He had hoped to write another, this one to

Bishop Germanus of Capua. God willing, every friend he had would be told of Placid's departure for Sicily and asked to pray for him. But there was more pressing business at hand. Agapitus needed cooking oil. Brother Michael, despite his vow of obedience, refused to give him any.

"I'll come at once," said the Abbot. And, as he followed Maurus to the kitchen, he thought upon the Rule he had written for the government of his monastery. Among other things, the Rule demanded that all guests be received as though they were Christ Himself. And no one in need was ever to be turned away.

Chapter 14

BROTHER MICHAEL AND
THE COOKING OIL

UNFORTUNATELY Brother Michael had forgotten all about the Rule. He could think of little else save that famine was threatening the whole of Italy. His voice was sharp as he addressed Agapitus.

"Didn't I tell you two days ago that we couldn't spare you any oil? Really, my friend, I'm surprised to see you back again today."

Agapitus was a young man, a student for the priesthood. Recently he had been raised to the rank of sub-deacon. Now he looked a little crestfallen as Brother Michael, in charge of food supplies at Monte Cassino, busied himself among the pots and pans.

"But Father Benedict told me to come back," he said slowly. "Don't you remember? He was quite upset when you sent me away empty-handed."

Brother Michael smiled grimly. Father Benedict was getting along in years. He was fifty-six years old now and far too holy to be a good businessman.

"These are hard times," he muttered. "There's a war going on. The Father Abbot, Lord bless him,

would give away all our food if I didn't watch out.
No, Agapitus. I'm sorry. You'll have to go elsewhere
for your oil."

Agapitus opened his mouth to explain his need
once more, then sighed. What was the use of argu-
ing with Brother Michael? "All right," he said
slowly. "I won't trouble you again."

As his visitor went out the door, Brother Michael
shoved a kettle over the fire with unusual vim. He
was trying hard not to be uncharitable, but there
were so many people like Agapitus. Not a day
passed that beggars didn't appear at his kitchen
door to ask for food. They were hungry, of course,
the innocent victims of the wartime food shortage,
but they were a nuisance, too.

"We've simply got to draw the line somewhere,"
thought Brother Michael. "That Agapitus, for
instance. Why didn't he take the time to cultivate
some good olive trees? Then he wouldn't have to go
begging for oil now. But that's the way with some
people. They never look ahead to the future. They
don't know the meaning of thrift."

While Brother Michael was congratulating himself upon his own good sense, the door to the
kitchen opened suddenly and the Abbot appeared
on the threshold. His eyes, as he glanced briefly
about the room, were troubled.

"Isn't Agapitus here, Brother Michael?"

The latter shook his head. "He just left, Father
Abbot. If you look through the window, you'll see
him going down the path."

Benedict strode into the kitchen, looked briefly

through the open window, then turned a stern glance on his disciple. "But he's going away empty-handed! What's the meaning of this? Brother Maurus told me the good man came to get the oil I promised him."

Brother Michael shifted uncomfortably. "I saw no reason to help him out, Father Abbot, especially when our own supply is so low. After all, he's a rather careless fellow . . ."

Benedict made a motion for silence. "How much oil have we left?"

The monk found a small bottle, which he had been careful to hide away two days ago, and presented it to his superior. "That's all, Father Abbot. You can see for yourself it isn't enough for our own needs."

Benedict went quickly to the door. "Brother Maurus!" he called. "Will you come here at once?"

Maurus entered the kitchen promptly, for he had been waiting just outside. "Yes, Father Abbot?"

Before the horrified gaze of Brother Michael, Benedict gave his young assistant the bottle of oil. "Throw this out the window," he commanded sternly. "We want no provisions in the house that are the result of disobedience."

The kitchen was built at the edge of a steep cliff. Brother Michael groaned inwardly as he thought of the jagged rocks below. But though he strained his ears to catch the sound of crashing glass, he heard nothing save the murmur of the wind rushing up from the valley and the harsh cries of blackbirds passing overhead.

Presently a little hope stole into his heart. "Thanks be to God, Father Abbot! I don't think the bottle broke. If you'll give me permission, I'll go down and see."

Benedict did not deign to answer. Bidding Maurus accompany him to the oratory, he turned on his heel and went quickly out the door.

But he was back in half an hour, accompanied this time by several other monks. As Brother Michael stared at this unusual assembly in the kitchen, uneasiness filled his heart. There was no doubt about it. Father Benedict was really angry that Agapitus had been sent away empty-handed.

Presently a hush fell upon the gathering. All eyes were on the Abbot and on Brother Maurus, who stood at his side. The latter seemed to have made a recent trip down the mountainside. Bits of twigs and leaves were still clinging to his habit, and his face was flushed from exertion.

"Well, Brother Maurus? What have you to report?"

The young monk felt in his sleeve and brought out a small object. "The bottle didn't break, Father Abbot. The oil didn't spill, either. I made sure before I left the place."

Brother Michael heaved a sigh of relief. This was nothing short of a miracle!

The Abbot took the bottle quietly. Then, turning to two young Oblates who stood close by, he bade them hurry to the house where Agapitus lived. They were to give him the bottle of oil with the Abbot's compliments. They were to say that Monte

Cassino welcomed all needy folk as though they were Christ Himself. If Agapitus wanted anything else, he was not to be afraid to come and state his case.

When the Oblates had disappeared on their errand, Benedict turned to Brother Michael. The latter, now very red in the face, scarcely raised his eyes.

"I see you're ashamed," said Benedict quietly. "And well you might be, Brother. You've been guilty of great unkindness to another human being."

There was silence for a moment. Then the Abbot turned to another monk. "Tell me what you promised when you came to this place," he said. "And speak out clearly, Brother. I want everyone to hear you."

The monk cast a brief glance at his unfortunate companion, then looked squarely at the Abbot. "I promised to stay in the monastery for life, unless you ordered me elsewhere, Father Abbot."

"And then?"

"I promised to change my worldly ways and strive for perfection."

"Lastly?"

"I promised obedience to you, Father Abbot, and to my other superiors."

Benedict nodded. "I'm glad you remember so well," he said. "Perhaps you remember these things, too, Brother Michael? Particularly the last part?"

Brother Michael took a deep breath. "Yes, Father Abbot. I remember them."

There was silence in the kitchen as the monks waited for Benedict to continue. But the Abbot lifted his hand in a sign that the meeting was over. "Return to your work," he ordered quietly. "As for you, Brother Michael, perhaps you'd better go to your cell and think upon the three things you promised when you came here? Particularly the matter of obedience?"

Brother Michael nodded. "Yes, Father Abbot," he said, and hastily took his place in the long line of monks filing out of the kitchen.

When he found himself alone, the Abbot looked about him silently. The monastery kitchen was a large place, kept neat and shining through the efforts of Brother Michael.

"Poor soul!" thought the Abbot. "I guess I gave him quite a scolding."

As he reflected that Brother Michael had not meant to forget the Rule, a wave of compassion swept into Benedict's heart. He crossed the room to where stood a large barrel. It was the barrel that should be full of oil but which now was empty, due to the fact that so much had been given to the poor.

The Abbot knelt down. "Dear Lord, have pity on Your servants!" he prayed. "Don't let us want for the necessities of life!"

As he addressed the Heavenly Father in tones of complete confidence, Benedict lost all track of time. It was only later, when he arose from his knees, that he noticed what had happened. Through God's mercy, the great barrel was no longer empty. Oil had gushed up from the bottom in a miraculous manner. Now it was even starting to overflow.

"God be praised!" cried Benedict, tears of joy springing to his eyes. "Won't Brother Michael be pleased about this!"

Chapter 15

FATHER OF THE POOR

A S THE months passed, conditions throughout Italy became worse. Taxes were high. Most young men had enlisted in the army of the Ostrogoths. Agriculture was neglected and famine resulted. Even at Monte Cassino, where Benedict and his monks remained aloof from war, there was a scarcity of food. Yet needy men and women flocked there to beg for food and clothing. Remembering the case of Brother Michael, the monks were most generous to everyone. Never was a person turned away empty-handed. As a result, layfolk in the neighborhood came to regard the Abbot as their loyal friend. There was nothing he would not do to help a person in trouble.

One morning a little group of people, residents of Casinum, stood talking about their beloved Benedict. "The good soul can do anything," said a young man in awed tones. "Yesterday he even cured a leper. Did you hear about it?"

An old man nodded vigorously. "Of course I heard about it. But did you hear about this? Last week I needed twelve shillings to pay a debt. I went to the Abbot and told him all about it. The good soul couldn't help me just then, but he promised to pray and said I was not to worry. The man to whom I owed the money wouldn't harm me, despite all his threats."

"And was the Abbot right?"

"Of course he was right. I came back to the monastery in two days as he told me to do, and what do you suppose happened?"

Someone laughed. "Why, Father Benedict gave you the twelve shillings. You paid your debt and everything was settled."

The man shook his head. "Father Benedict did better than that. He gave me *thirteen* shillings— enough money to pay my creditor and still have a shilling for myself. He said he had found the money in a very strange place—on top of the corn bin. But he couldn't explain how it got there."

"I know a better story than that," cried a woman suddenly. "It happened just the other day."

Her husband nodded. "We'd run short of bread," he explained. "When we went to the monastery and explained that we had six children, the good Abbot and his monks insisted on giving us a loaf for each."

"Yes, even though by that time they had only five loaves left for themselves," put in the wife. "But Father Benedict insisted five loaves were plenty for the monks and himself."

"*Plenty?* For more than three hundred men and boys?"

"That's what he said. And I heard him comforting young Brother Matthew with these words: 'Why are you sad for lack of bread? There is want today, but tomorrow you shall have plenty.'"

"That's right," continued the husband. "I heard those words, too. And because I didn't believe them, and because I felt ashamed for having taken six loaves, I went back to the monastery the next day to return two of them to Father Benedict. Only in the meantime . . ."

"Only in the meantime another wonder had happened," put in the woman happily. "During the night an unknown person left two hundred bushels of meal at the monastery gate. There was no longer a shortage of flour. As a result, Father Benedict made us take home the bread we wanted to return. He even gave us six more loaves, and a special blessing for ourselves and our children."

While the people of Casinum were thus peacefully discussing Benedict's kindness, an unhappy scene was taking place a mile or so away. A local peasant had had the bad fortune to meet his creditor, a rough barbarian named Zalla. The latter, mounted on his horse, was now threatening the poor man's life if he did not pay his debt at once.

"You have gold hidden some place!" shouted Zalla, dealing the peasant a stinging blow with his whip. "Come on, you wretched fool—hand it over to me!"

The latter cringed. "I haven't any gold," he whimpered. "Please believe me!"

Zalla laughed coarsely. He was a rough, hairy man, an Arian heretic, who delighted in plaguing Catholics. Already he had killed several of them,

and now his brutal heart rejoiced at the sight of
still another victim.

"So you're not going to talk, eh?"

The peasant swallowed hard. "Just give me a little time and I'll pay everything I owe. Honestly I
will! But right now . . ."

"Well? Speak up, fool! Right now what?"

The peasant offered a brief prayer, then summoned all his courage. "Right now I've given my
money to Father Benedict for safekeeping. I haven't
a penny with me or at home."

"That's a likely story!"

"But it's true. Just ask Father Benedict!"

Zalla flicked his whip aimlessly. Perhaps the foolish peasant spoke the truth. Perhaps he had given
his money to the Abbot of Monte Cassino. With a
grunt he leaped from his horse and seized his victim in an iron grip.

"If you're telling a lie, it'll go hard with you!" he
roared. "Here, put your arms behind your back.
And don't think you can escape. I'm going to bind
you with a good stout cord and take you to this
monk."

The peasant stood shivering as the rough barbarian tied his hands. The cord cut into his flesh,
but he dared make no sound. Zalla would have
tortured him even more.

Presently the barbarian mounted his horse and
bade the peasant lead him to the monastery. The
latter, overcome with fear, nodded weakly and
began to stumble forward in the direction of Monte
Cassino. Occasionally his oppressor dealt him a

blow with his whip, taunting him with insults and bidding him move along faster.

"I'm going to die!" thought the unhappy peasant. "Oh, God of the Christians, be merciful! The Abbot Benedict doesn't know me at all! What will he do when Zalla asks for my money?"

When an hour had passed, the suffering man found himself at Monte Cassino. Dusty and covered with blood, he managed to stagger to the gate. A solitary figure, clad in the garb of a monk, was sitting there reading. The peasant pointed weakly.

"There he is," he said. "That's the Abbot Benedict."

Zalla let out a great roar. He was accustomed to getting what he wanted by this means, and there was no reason to believe the method would not succeed now. He dug his spurs into the horse's flanks and rushed toward the silent figure.

"You there, you monk!" he cried. "Get up! Give back what you've taken from this fool or I'll break every bone in your body!"

Benedict looked up from his reading. He seemed quite unconcerned at Zalla's terrifying appearance, at the heavy whip in his hand, the evil fire that burned in his eyes. Instead, he looked long and kindly at the frightened peasant.

There was something peculiar in that look. Zalla turned a curious eye on his victim, then clutched his own throat fearfully. The stout cord that held the peasant's arms was beginning to unwind of itself, and so speedily that the latter was free in a single instant. Overcome at the wondrous sight, Zalla slipped from his horse and groveled in the dust at Benedict's feet. His heart was beating wildly. Who was this grey-haired man who could work such wonders?

"Have mercy, Father Abbot!" he begged. "Don't put a curse on me!"

Benedict said nothing. He did not even look at Zalla. Instead, he reached out a kindly hand to the trembling peasant and bade him go into the monastery. The monks would give him food and drink. They would also care for his wounds.

"You could tell Brother Maurus I wish to see him," he added. "And don't be afraid, my son. This man will never harm you again."

A few hours later the peasant said good-bye to Benedict and his monks. He felt like a new person. There was no fear in his heart now. He had the Abbot's promise that Zalla was going to reform.

"It's too good to be true," he told himself. "Imagine Zalla becoming a Catholic!"

The peasant walked down the mountain road singing a happy song. Suddenly he caught sight of a familiar figure. It was his old friend Paul. He hadn't seen Paul for many weeks, and so he hurried forward to tell him of the day's wonderful events. "Father Benedict is the greatest man in Italy!" he cried. "Good old friend, if you had seen Zalla, as I did, lying in the dust and crying for mercy, you'd say the world is a pretty good place after all!"

Paul nodded. But he didn't seem too surprised. "Look over there," he said presently. "What do you see?"

"HAVE MERCY, FATHER ABBOT!" HE BEGGED.
"DON'T PUT A CURSE ON ME!"

The peasant shaded his eyes. "It's a boy gathering wood," he said. "Your boy, isn't he?"

The man nodded. "Don't talk to me of wonders, old friend. Last week that little lad was dead."

The peasant gasped. "You don't mean . . ."

"I mean just that. I brought that little body, limp and lifeless, to Father Benedict. The good man said some prayers. Within an hour my son was strong and well again."

The peasant made an awkward Sign of the Cross. It was a gesture he had learned from the Abbot and his monks just an hour ago—an introduction to the Christian religion his whole heart was now yearning to embrace.

Chapter 16

BROTHER JOSEPH
AND THE HANDKERCHIEFS

A S THE years passed, Benedict's fame grew. His monastery on Monte Cassino, "The School of the Lord's Service," was now an immense household of men and boys. The monastery at Terracina was also prospering, and many noblemen renounced all their wealth to seek God in these two monasteries Benedict had founded.

Sometimes the Abbot was sorely distressed at the fame that was his. He recalled his youthful ambition to be a hermit, to serve God far from the distractions and flattery of men. At such times he looked long and hard at the seventh chapter of the Rule he had written. Here were set forth the merits of one of his favorite virtues—humility. Years ago he had written that humility is a ladder to Heaven. By climbing from one rung to the next, a man can become a saint. He can learn to do without earthly pleasures and find his supreme joy in God.

The monks and Oblates listened carefully to Benedict's frequent talks on the virtue of humility. They also studied the Rule the Abbot had written, "a little Rule for beginners," as he called it. There were seventy-three short chapters and an introduction. Possibly because of the troubled times in which Benedict was living, the hidden theme of his Rule was peace. The monks and Oblates were cautioned to be at peace with themselves and with one another. Those in authority were not to be suspicious. Everyone in the monastery was to remember that the Three Persons of the Most Blessed Trinity dwell in peaceful hearts. A soul in the state of grace is the temple of God, entitled to respect and kindness.

Despite the fact that the Rule was read daily to the assembled community, human nature was not reformed overnight. One afternoon, as Benedict was going to work in the fields, he saw Brother Joseph coming hastily toward him. The Abbot smiled briefly. Brother Joseph was a good man, but he was due for a scolding just the same. That morning, through carelessness, he had broken a very important part of the Rule.

"You sent for me, Father Abbot?"

Benedict surveyed his disciple gravely. "This morning you left the monastery grounds."

Brother Joseph nodded. "Yes, Father Abbot. I went to give a little sermon to the nuns at Saint Helen's convent. You asked me to do that last night."

At these words the Abbot's face became surprisingly stern. "How is it that evil has entered your heart, Brother? How is it you can stand here and face me as though you had done no wrong?"

Poor Brother Joseph stared in dismay. He could

not think of any wrong he had done. After all, the
Abbot had told him to preach a sermon to the nuns.
He had obeyed the command, then returned
directly to Monte Cassino. Saint Helen's convent
was only two miles away and the trip had not taken
long.

"I'm sorry if I've displeased you, Father Abbot,"
he stammered. "Please forgive me!"

Benedict felt inclined to smile, to finish quickly
with this test of Brother Joseph's humility. Yet
something told him to continue the questioning a
little longer.

"So you think you did nothing wrong this
morning?"

"I must have, Father Abbot. Otherwise you
wouldn't be so angry."

"But you can't remember?"

"No, Father Abbot. I can't remember a thing."

At these words Benedict relented. Looking upon
the monk with steady gentleness, he asked him if
he could repeat from memory the Rule by which the
monastery was governed. A smile of relief lit up
Brother Joseph's anxious features. He had lived on
Monte Cassino for twelve years. He knew every
word of the Rule by heart. As he started to recite
the opening paragraph, however, Benedict suggested he confine himself to one part of the Rule
only—the fifty-fourth chapter.

"And speak slowly and distinctly, Brother, so that
the meaning of the words will be clear to you."

Brother Joseph nodded, and after a moment's
hesitation began to quote the desired chapter.

"On no account shall it be lawful for a monk to receive either from his parents or anyone else, or from his brethren, letters, presents or any little gifts, without the permission of his Abbot. And if anything be sent to him, even by his parents, let him not presume to receive it, except it first shall have been shown to the Abbot. If he order it to be received, it shall be in the Abbot's power to command to whom it shall be given; and let not the brother to whom it has been sent be grieved, lest occasion be given to the Devil . . ."

The Abbot listened quietly to Brother Joseph's accurate recital of the Rule. When deep crimson suddenly flooded the latter's face, a little smile flickered on Benedict's lips.

"Well, Brother? You remember your fault now?"

The monk, deeply confused, put his hand into the front of his habit and drew forth a small package. "This morning the nuns at the convent gave me some handkerchiefs," he stammered. "Believe me, Father Abbot, I'd forgotten all about them!"

Benedict smiled. "It's all right, Brother Joseph. The good sisters meant well. But you should have come and told me about this gift."

Brother Joseph nodded, and thrust the package into Benedict's hands. "Here they are, Father Abbot. And please forgive me!"

The Abbot examined the handkerchiefs carefully. They were made of very fine linen, neatly hemmed.

However, they seemed rather unsuited to a man who must spend much of his time working in the fields.

"Perhaps they'll make somebody happy," he said presently. "Brother Joseph, you may go down to the village and give these handkerchiefs to the first poor person you meet."

"Yes, Father Abbot," said the monk hastily. "I'll go to Casinum right away."

When the story of Brother Joseph and the hand-kerchiefs made the rounds at Monte Cassino, there was one monk who showed little surprise. This was Brother Valentinian.

"Our Father Abbot often knows what's going on in faraway places," he said. "Brother Joseph, didn't he give you any idea of this wonderful gift?"

The latter nodded. "He said to me these words: 'Was I not present when you took the handker-chiefs from God's handmaids?' Oh, my brother! May God forgive me that I so carelessly broke the holy Rule!"

Brother Valentinian smiled. "Don't worry too much," he said. "And let me tell you something. This business of the handkerchiefs reminds me of another wonder. You know my brother James?"

The monk nodded. "He was here visiting you last week."

"That's right. James comes to see me once a year. Though he doesn't seem to have the vocation to be a monk, he's strangely attracted to our monastery. And to Father Benedict. He always makes his trips here in the spirit of a pilgrim coming to a shrine,

never touching food or drink throughout the whole
day's journey."

"He must be a very devout soul."

"Devout? He certainly is. But last week, on the
way to see me, he met another traveler. This man
carried a package of food. The day was very hot and
presently he suggested to James that they stop a
while and have something to eat."

"And they did?"

Brother Valentinian smiled. "At first James
refused to eat anything, explaining that it was his
custom to go fasting to our Father Abbot. A second
time the stranger begged him to take a little food.
James still refused. But later on, when they came to
a little brook running through a pleasant meadow,
his hunger got the better of him. He agreed to share
the stranger's food and drink."

Brother Joseph laughed. "I can guess what happened when James reached our monastery."

"Of course you can. God's power had allowed
Father Abbot to see what was happening on the
journey. When James arrived here, late at night,
Father Abbot wouldn't give him his blessing. He
asked him how it was that the Devil, who had spoken through the mouth of a fellow traveler, had not
been able to make him break his fast at first, then
finally had succeeded."

"Your brother must have been surprised at such
words."

"Surprised? Brother Joseph, he was dumb-
founded! He got down on his knees and confessed
his weakness, shaking like a leaf because our

Father Abbot knew what had happened."

"Of course it really wasn't a sin to take food on that long journey"

"No, but Father Abbot was disappointed in James because he had thrown away a good opportunity to make up for his sins. He explained that this was just what the Devil wanted. The Devil is always trying to make us break our good resolutions. He gets us to think how tired we are. In the end we decide he is right and that our good deeds are too small to be important."

Brother Joseph agreed heartily with this statement. To grow weary in the long struggle for perfection was an ailment that afflicted all men, in monasteries and outside. The way to conquer such a feeling was to consider oneself a child, then to ask the Heavenly Father for strength and courage. Such a prayer must always be answered. The trouble was that few people ever thought of putting themselves in a child's place. Unconsciously they prided themselves on their own strength and knowledge. When these gave way, they became downhearted. Life was too hard, they told themselves. It was impossible to be a saint. They forgot that it is just when we feel most down-hearted that we have the best chance to practice great trust in God.

As the two exchanged a few thoughts on these matters, Brother Joseph remarked, "That reminds me of our faithful Brother Andrew."

"Ah, yes," replied Brother Valentinian. "Andrew was a wavering soul in his younger days.

Remember what he told us? How Father Abbot had
to keep listening to his pleading: 'O Father Abbot, I
don't want to be always obeying rules and taking
care of my soul? I want to go enjoy myself in the
world!'"

"Yes," answered Brother Joseph. "And Father
Abbot would always answer, 'God wants you to be
holy and happy by being a good monk, Andrew.
You must not desert your vocation.'"

Brother Joseph warmed to the story and continued. "One day, however, Andrew was so insistent
that Father Abbot angrily answered him, 'All right,
then! Be off with you!' So Andrew set out. But
scarcely had he gone far from the monastery when
he met a dragon heading straight toward him with
mouth wide open! The terrified Andrew cried out,
'Help! Help! This dragon is going to devour me!'
The monks heard his cries and ran out to help."

"But they didn't see any dragon!" put in Brother
Valentinian. "Nevertheless, they brought Andrew
back to the monastery, and there he promised to
stay."

"And he did stay," finished Brother Joseph. "Never
again did Andrew attempt to run away from his
calling."

"That's right," agreed Brother Valentinian.
"Andrew became a fine monk. Father Abbot's
prayers had won him the special grace to see the
dragon that he had been following around. Ah, that
was another victory our Father Abbot won over the
Evil One," he mused.

"And Brother Andrew has always been grateful

for that," added Brother James.

So the years passed, with life on the great mountain above Casinum continuing in orderly fashion. Benedict seldom left his monastery, save to visit the countryfolk of the neighborhood. His one concern was to help others, to be of comfort when the sword of sorrow struck. Did he dream that the time was close at hand for his own soul to be tried in suffering?

Chapter 17

KING TOTILA
TRIES TO FOOL THE ABBOT

IT WAS late in the autumn of 540, when he was
sixty years old, that the keen blade of sorrow
sought out the Abbot's heart. It came in a message from Sicily. Placid and his companions, who
recently had completed their monastery, had been
murdered by pirates. Only one monk, Brother
Gordian, had escaped with his life.

Benedict needed all his strength to bear up under
this great blow. Placid, the young disciple whom he
loved so much, had been tortured and put to death
by cruel barbarians! Thirty other monks had suf-
fered the same fate! The tragedy had occurred in
the early hours of the morning while the community was at prayer. More than that. Placid's sister
and two of his brothers, guests of the young superior, had been ordered from their beds and forced to
walk with the monks to the seashore. Here the
entire group had been cruelly murdered.

Brother Maurus was aghast at the news, for he
and Placid had been friends since childhood. They
had come to Subiaco on the same day. They had
grown to manhood under the watchful eye of the

120

kindly Abbot. Remembering these things, Maurus presently suggested that Benedict send him to Sicily to rebuild Placid's ruined monastery. He would not be afraid if the cruel pirates returned. God willing, he would teach them the truths of the Christian faith. He would make them understand that no man can be happy unless he loves all other men.

"You'll let me go, Father Abbot?"

Benedict shook his head. "No, my son," he said gently. "I have other work for you here. And don't be sad. Brother Placid and his friends are now glorious saints in Heaven. Through the merits of their martyrdom, they will obtain for us great blessings."

Yet the Abbot's heart was heavy, despite these cheerful words. The world was so full of sorrow! It was now five years since the legions of Justinian, under Belisarius, had arrived in Italy to wage war against the Ostrogoths. During this time thousands of young men had died in Italy. Other thousands— old men, women and children—had starved to death because of repeated famine. Even Rome, the great city that once had ruled the world, was in a state of decay. Everywhere greedy men watched their neighbors slyly, hoping for a chance to seize power for themselves. Only a handful of Christians bothered to think of the Ten Commandments. In truth, it was a sad hour for civilization.

"God be merciful!" Benedict prayed. "Teach us the peace of Your holy saints! Teach us to love one another! And teach us to forgive our enemies!"

Although the Abbot was a famous man by now, he had not many companions in such prayers. In cities and towns men were concentrating on more worldly matters. How were taxes to be raised to pay for the war? What about those rumors that the bubonic plague was creeping steadily closer to Italy? And what about the huge numbers of crippled soldiers coming back to their families? How were they to earn a living once again?

Although he saw no way out of the difficulty, Benedict continued to work and pray. By now Monte Cassino had become an island of peace in a troubled sea. Children were educated and taught useful trades in the monastery school. Daily the Word of God was preached in the oratory. Needy families were cared for in a spirit of love. The homeless, the sick, even the insane, were given shelter and food. And in the silent cloister of the monastery, patient monks translated and copied hundreds of manuscripts so that the lamp of learning would not be extinguished in the darkness of war.

Word of such events finally reached the ears of King Totila, leader of the Ostrogoth armies. Although Totila was a barbarian, he had a secret admiration for the man of Monte Cassino, the hero of the hills who fought no wars and yet influenced hundreds of lives.

"I'm going to see this monk," Totila announced one day. "The war is going well with us. I can afford a little rest."

Totila's followers were not too eager to visit Monte Cassino. They had heard all manner of

stories about the Abbot. Hadn't he raised the dead
to life and cured hundreds of hopeless invalids?
More than that. Couldn't he read the secret
thoughts of others at will?

"Do not go, sire!" begged Totila's followers. "This
Christian monk cries out against war. Perhaps he'll
put a spell on you so that you can never fight
again!"

"Nonsense!" cried Totila. "Let it never be said I
fear any man. Make ready for our trip."

So, late in the year 542, a strange procession set
out for Monte Cassino. It was composed of a select
group of Totila's best warriors, mounted on fiery
horses and bearing their swords and spears. At the
head of the procession rode the King, dressed in the
rich purple that proclaimed his rank.

"I can hardly wait to see this monk," he told himself. "From all accounts he's a real wonderworker.
But maybe it would be better to let him know I'm
coming. It would be too bad if he weren't at the
monastery when I arrived."

So a message was sent to the Abbot, stating that
the King of the Ostrogoths was about to pay him a
visit. At once Benedict sent a reply saying Totila
would be most welcome.

As the latter listened to the Abbot's message (he
himself had never learned to read or write), the
thought occurred to him that it would be most
interesting to see whether Benedict were a real
prophet or not.

"Riggo!" cried the King suddenly. "I want you to
wear my robes and ride my horse!"

Riggo, a rough barbarian who served in the King's bodyguard, could hardly believe his ears. He, an ordinary soldier, was to wear the royal purple of a king? Yet he dared not make any comment.

"Yes, sire," he said quickly. And in a few minutes he had exchanged his soldier's garb for the royal garments of his master.

But the King was not satisfied. "You're to go to Monte Cassino in my place, Riggo. We want to see if this monk is all that people say he is. But you must look like a real king. Here, take my sword. And let Vultheric, Ruderic and Blidi act as your bodyguard."

Riggo nodded. He was beginning to understand Totila's plan. But he was a little nervous. Suppose this monk suspected that a trick was being played on him? What would happen then? Perhaps he would be dreadfully angry. Perhaps he would order Riggo to be tortured and killed.

"I'll do my best to act like a king, sire," he said in a low voice. "Believe me!"

Totila laughed heartily. "This is going to be good," he declared. "Hurry up, Riggo. Bear the compliments of King Totila to the Abbot of Monte Cassino."

So Riggo set out, flanked by his bodyguard and followed by a hundred picked soldiers. As the group advanced up the winding mountain road, it presented a striking sight. The steel helmets, swords and spears shone with dazzling brilliance in the sun. The colored standards of the little company waved proudly in the breeze. And the horses, strong and of the best stock, reared their heads and pranced like the thoroughbreds they were.

First to behold the glittering spectacle was a group of monks working in the fields. Hastily they ran to warn Benedict of Totila's approach.

"He's coming, Father Abbot!" they cried. "And he has many others with him."

The Abbot nodded calmly. "I'm ready," he said.

As Riggo entered the monastery gates, he found his former anxiety giving way to a state of pleasant excitement. It was good to wear fine clothes, to have many men paying him deference. It was also good to feel the King's sword resting easily in his hand. By now he felt sure that he was playing his part well, and he made up his mind to be quite composed while talking with the Abbot. It might even be possible so to impress the monk with his power that the latter would make him some fine present.

Presently Riggo and his party arrived at the very doors of the monastery. The barbarian looked about impatiently. Only one monk was in evidence. This was a meek-looking man in his early sixties, quietly seated under a tree. He made no effort to rise, calmly observing the gorgeous procession before him.

"Where's the monk Benedict?" roared Riggo, riding up to the latter with a flourish. "King Totila is here and wishes to pay his respects."

The solitary monk, who was really the Abbot, smiled quietly.

"Put off those robes, my son. They are not yours."

Riggo stiffened. *"What?"*

"HURRY UP, RIGGO. BEAR THE COMPLIMENTS OF
KING TOTILA TO THE ABBOT OF MONTE CASSINO."

"Your King is not here. He is a mile away, waiting to hear about this little trick. Ah, my sons, did you really think you'd fool me?"

Riggo and the soldiers stared in terror. Of a sudden those nearest the end of the line wheeled their horses and galloped frantically through the gate. Riggo watched them go, then looked hopelessly at the sword in his hand. He had not the strength to lift it. He looked at Vultheric, Ruderic, Blidi—the strong men who had been appointed as his bodyguard. Their faces were pale as death, their hands shaking as though with palsy. Quietly the would-be King slipped from his horse and prostrated himself in the dust. Those of his company who still remained did likewise.

Benedict smiled. "Don't be afraid," he said gently. "Tell your King, when you return to him, that he is still welcome at Monte Cassino. But tell him, too, not to be so cruel in battle. The sword of sorrow is a deadly weapon, my friends. The fruit is bitter for all concerned."

Chapter 18

BENEDICT TELLS A STORY

RIGGO was not long in giving Totila the Abbot's message. When the latter learned that Benedict was really a prophet, that he had been able to see through the trick played upon him, he was stricken with fear.

"What shall I do?" he asked his counselors anxiously. "This man really possesses great powers."

The counselors could not agree upon what to do. Finally King Totila put an end to the argument. He would go to Monte Cassino after all. He, the mighty king of the Ostrogoths, who one day would conquer Naples and Rome, would make his apologies to a simple monk.

Totila arrived quite humbly at Benedict's monastery. A short distance from the gates he dismounted, then walked slowly into the grounds. When he saw the grey-haired monk his followers had described as the Abbot, still sitting under a tree, he threw himself flat on his face. His heart was pounding wildly, and if he had not been a brave man he would have fled at once. Yet he remained prostrate, waiting for the Abbot to speak.

"Rise, my son," called Benedict promptly, realizing

that the real king had arrived at last. But though
he repeated his words more than once, Totila stayed
in the same position. He seemed like some poor
beast of burden, beaten by its master and afraid to
lift its head. Finally the Abbot arose and went to
the trembling man. Gently he helped him to his
feet. Then, in kindly words, he began to reprove
him for his cruel treatment of prisoners, the many
innocent people he had put to the sword.

"Don't you know the meaning of love?" he asked.
"Don't you know that all men are brothers, created
for the Kingdom of Christ? Believe me, there is no
happiness for one who forgets these things."

Totila listened humbly, begged pardon of the
Abbot for the trick he had played, then asked for
prayers. The latter smiled.

"Prayers, my son? What good are they if you fail
to change your ways?"

Totila shifted uneasily. "But I'm a man of war,
Father Abbot. I'm trying to defend our country
against this foreigner, the Emperor of Justinian.
How can I be kind to those who would kill me if
they could?"

Benedict was silent for a moment. Then he laid a
kindly hand upon Totila's shoulder. "All I ask is
that you be merciful," he said finally. "Take cap-
tives, if you must, but remember that each of these
poor creatures bears within him an immortal soul.
That soul is made in the image of God. You have no
right to insult it, to torture the body in which it
dwells."

A glimmer of admiration flickered in the King's

eyes. The Abbot's Christian kindness, his straight-
forward words, were slowly making a deep impression. "I'll try to be merciful," he muttered. "Only
please pray for me, Father Abbot. Everyone says
that you work wonders with your prayers."

A shadow of sadness passed across the monk's
face. "I'll pray for you, my son, since that is my duty
as your brother. But there's another reason, too.
Only nine more years will be given you to reign
over Italy. In the tenth you will die, in a land
across the sea."

Sudden fear clutched at Totila's heart. "Oh, no,
Father Abbot! Not that! Don't tell me I'm going to
die!"

Benedict smiled. "A just man has no fear of death,
my son. Remember that when you are once more on
the battlefield, when great cities fall before your
armies and all men pay you honor."

Totila nodded silently. His heart had suddenly
lost its eagerness for further words with the Abbot.
Ten more years of life! It was a miserably short
time.

"Thank you," he stammered. "Father Abbot, I'll
never forget this visit."

As the King turned to leave the monastery
grounds, Benedict raised his hand in gentle blessing. In some mysterious way he knew that from now
on Totila would be a better man—more merciful in
war, more just in peace.

A few days after Benedict's meeting with Totila,
another group of important visitors arrived on
Monte Cassino. They were priests and laymen from

France, and in their hands they bore letters of introduction from the Bishop of Le Mans. They had come to beg the Abbot for some missionaries. Could he spare a few monks to open a monastery at Glanfeuil, a town in the province of Anjou?

It was now slightly more than two years since the martyrdom of Placid and his companions in Sicily. Benedict thought long and hard about the prospect of sending more of his sons into a foreign land.

"But France is quite different from Sicily," said the members of the delegation. "Father Abbot, we have few barbarians in our country. Your monks will be perfectly safe at Glanfeuil."

The Abbot nodded. "I understand," he said. "You have few barbarians but you do have heretics."

"Arian heretics, Father Abbot. There are thousands of them."

For a moment Benedict was silent. Seven years ago he had sent his beloved Placid to Sicily. Now there was no doubt that God was asking still another sacrifice. Of all the monks at Monte Cassino, none was better suited to head the new foundation in France than Brother Maurus. The latter was wise, holy, and experienced in leading others to perfection. He was thirty-two years old. Almost since boyhood he had assisted the Abbot in affairs concerning the monastery. For a while he had even had complete charge of the monks at Subiaco.

"Let me think a little while," Benedict told the Bishop's messengers. "In the meantime, make yourselves at home in our monastery. Brother Timothy will care for your needs in the guest house."

For a few days the Abbot prayed for light and thought over the idea of opening a new house for his monks in France. Finally he sent for Brother Maurus. When the latter arrived, Benedict bade him be seated.

"I want to tell you a story," he said. "Listen well, my brother, even though my words may not be new to you."

Maurus nodded. Had there ever been a time when he had failed to pay attention to the holy man who was his Abbot?

"About forty-six years ago," began Benedict, "France was a rather wild country. It was ruled by King Clovis, a pagan."

Maurus smiled. He had learned as much history before coming to Subiaco.

"Well, Clovis married a Christian princess from Burgundy. Her name was Clotildis. Because the King loved her so much, he agreed that their children might be baptized and brought up as Catholics. And so it was done. Often Clotildis prayed that her husband would become a Christian, but her prayers seemed to go unanswered. Clovis had little use for religion, although he did not interfere with his wife's spiritual duties."

Maurus nodded. He had heard this story, too, but not for worlds would he interrupt the Abbot.

"In 496 a wild tribe of barbarians, the Allemanni, crossed the Rhine and invaded France. At once Clovis set out to protect his people. But before he left, his wife cautioned him in these words:

'My lord, to be victorious invoke the God of the Christians. He is the sole Lord of the world and is called the God of battles. If you call on Him with confidence, nothing can resist you!'

"Clovis promised to remember these words, although he was quite sure his armies would be successful. But the Allemanni were better warriors than anyone expected. Very soon Clovis was forced to change his opinion, to admit that his own forces were in great danger. One day, while his men were dying by the thousands, he cried out in desperation: 'Oh, Christ, Whom Clotildis invokes as Son of the Living God, I implore Thy help! I have called upon my gods and they have no power! I therefore call upon Thee! I believe in Thee! Deliver me from my enemies and I will be baptized in Thy Name!'"

For a moment the Abbot was silent, gazing into space as though he would recall those far-off days when he had been a sixteen-year-old student and Clovis was fighting the fierce Allemanni. But presently he turned again to Maurus.

"Forgive an old man's ramblings, my son. You know this story as well as I do. Let me hear you finish it."

Maurus smiled. "Clovis won the battle, Father Abbot, and the Allemanni went back to their own country. And when the King returned to his wife, he was very humble. He said: 'Clovis has vanquished the Allemanni and you have triumphed over Clovis. What you have so much at heart is done at last.'"

"And what did the Queen say?"

"She replied: 'To the God of Hosts is the glory of both these triumphs due.'"

"And then?"

"Then the Queen took her husband to the good Remigius, Bishop of Reims. After being instructed in our holy Faith, he was baptized on Christmas Day of that same year, 496. The streets were decorated with gay flags. Three thousand of Clovis' soldiers also were baptized, and many women and children. From then until now France has been a Catholic country."

"With the exception of some heretics, Brother Maurus."

The younger monk nodded. "Yes, Father Abbot. I guess there are many of those."

For a while the Abbot and his young disciple talked further of conditions in France, of the holy man Remigius, dead since 535, who had baptized Clovis and done so much to Christianize his native land. When the bell finally sounded for Vespers, Maurus' eyes were shining. The conversation with the Abbot could have only one meaning. He was to go to France. Like Placid before him, his duty was to bring the word of God to ignorant souls.

It was a few days later that the Abbot confirmed this hope. Maurus was to go to Glanfeuil to superintend the building of the new monastery. He would have four companions—Simplicius, Antonius, Constantinianus and Faustus—all wise and holy men. The group would leave Monte Cassino on the tenth day of January.

When the great hour finally arrived, the Abbot

gave an inspiring talk to the little group of missionaries. Then, drawing Maurus aside, he placed a kindly hand upon his shoulder.

"I have a little gift for you," he said. "Take it, my son. And whenever you look upon it, pray for Benedict, a sinner."

The gift proved to be a copy of the Rule in Benedict's own handwriting. There were other gifts, too, but the Abbot made no mention of these. He had arranged to give them to a messenger who would overtake the departing missionaries when they had gone a day's journey. One of these gifts was a box of relics. The other was a letter of encouragement to Maurus and his companions. Among other things the letter prophesied that Maurus would govern the new monastery in France for thirty-eight years. Then he would retire to a hermit's cell. He would die shortly afterward, at the age of seventy-two. The letter also foretold Benedict's own death within the space of four years.

Chapter 19

THE PASSING YEARS

WHEN Maurus and his companions disappeared down the winding mountain road for the last time, Benedict hastened to his cell to pray for them. This cell was really a stone tower, once part of the fortifications built on Monte Cassino by Roman soldiers. It was divided into two rooms, one above the other, connected by a stairway. In the lower half of the tower Benedict was accustomed to read, write and receive visitors. The upper half he used as an oratory. Each night he would go there, while his monks took their well-earned rest, to speak to God and reflect upon the beauties of Heaven.

Having gained the seclusion of this upper room, Benedict knelt down. It seemed impossible that he would not see his beloved Maurus again. But it was true. Already the young monk and his companions had begun the long trip to France. Only Faustus and Simplicius would ever return to Monte Cassino. "Dear Lord, accept this sacrifice of my children," Benedict prayed. "Give them strength and courage for the trials that lie ahead."

As he prayed, other thoughts crept into the

Abbot's mind. He recalled Placid's martyrdom in
Sicily. He thought of another good friend, Bishop
Germanus of Capua, now happy in Heaven for
almost two years. Through the goodness of God, he
had been privileged to see the Bishop's soul entering Paradise. The wonder had taken place at night,
in this very room. Abbot Servandus, who lived in a
neighboring monastery, had been sleeping in the
lower room at the time. Benedict had called him to
come and see the great vision. The whole night sky
was ablaze with mysterious light. In the midst of
the radiance, the earth seemed to take form in one
of the rays.

"I was able to see the whole world and all its
peoples at the same time," Benedict thought. "Ah,
Lord! How good You were to me that night! You let
me know that men would continue to live under my
Rule until the end of time!"

As he knelt there, reflecting upon these and
other blessings, the Abbot's thoughts turned back
to the time when he had mended the sieve for
Cyrilla, then fled away to be a hermit at Subiaco.
Life had been peaceful among the hills. Yet there
had been a day when he had weakened in his
efforts to be a saint. While living in his cave, cold
and hungry, a violent temptation had tortured him.
An inner voice had ridiculed the hardships in a
hermit's life. It had pointed out the many pleasures
a man could enjoy in Rome. Rightful pleasures,
too—the joy of having a home and children, of
being honored by one's fellows.

"But You helped me, Lord!" thought Benedict.

"You inspired me to take upon myself some kind of suffering, so that I would forget such thoughts. There was a clump of nettles near my cave. I threw myself into them and the pain made me forget all about the temptation. When I finally arose, torn and bleeding, I had no wish but to continue serving You in prayer and sacrifice. And how glad I am now that You helped me with Your grace! For I would have been very unhappy at Rome. The only thing I ever enjoyed there was the chance to visit the Catacombs."

Life on Monte Cassino continued in the same orderly fashion after Maurus' departure for France. Additional men and boys came to Benedict to be monks and Oblates. War still ravaged Italy, and hardship was everywhere, but the monks of Monte Cassino remained the champions of the poor. With few exceptions, they were the only educated men in the whole country who believed that manual labor was not a mark of low social standing. Embraced in the proper spirit, they insisted it could be of great help to both soul and body. It was also a way to attain humility—that wonderful ladder that ends at the Throne of God in Heaven.

"If only more people would believe this!" Benedict often thought. "The war would stop if they realized that we are all brothers, created to be one in Christ—headed for Heaven but making a detour in this world. But no. Success continues to be measured by wealth, power, honor. One man is always setting himself over another. Even in prayer there is rebellion. People want to pray only for themselves. They don't want to pray for one another. What would happen, I wonder, if the whole human race decided to follow God's Will and become one family in Christ?"

Benedict did not really have to wonder about this. Well he knew what would be the result of such a miracle. Hatred and envy would disappear. There would be no more wars. Earth would become a little Paradise.

Chapter 20

A VISION OF THE FUTURE

ALTHOUGH war had been ravaging Italy for nearly ten years, the spirit of peace was thoroughly cultivated in the monastery. Seven times a day, beginning at two o'clock in the morning, the Abbot and his monks gathered as a family to offer praise to God. The prayers were not the selection of any individual. They were the Psalms, written thousands of years ago by King David. As soon as a boy arrived at Monte Cassino to become an Oblate, he was set to learning these Psalms. There was no more important work, said the Abbot, than the reverent recital of these ancient prayers.

So the years passed. Important men still continued to come from Rome and Naples to ask the Abbot's prayers and counsel. Another regular visitor was Sabinus, Bishop of Canusium, a town in southeast Italy. Sabinus agreed heartily with all Benedict's ideals. One day, late in December of 546, the two sat talking in the lower room of Benedict's tower. A few days before, King Totila had succeeded in defeating the Emperor's armies. The city of Rome was now in his hands.

"Alas!" cried the Bishop. "Rome will be destroyed by this barbarian king! Never again will it be a fit dwelling for men!"

Benedict smiled sadly. "Rome will not be destroyed by the barbarians. It will be worn out by tempest, lightning, whirlwind and earthquake. It will decay in itself."

Sabinus sighed. "What fools men are! Why can't they realize that peace with God and man is the secret of happiness? Good friend, you have put things well in your Rule. *Turn away from evil and do good. Seek after peace and pursue it.*' What wise words those are!"

"But really not my own, Your Lordship. You must have guessed that I borrowed them from the thirty-third Psalm."

The Bishop nodded. Even as they spoke, the bell was ringing to summon Benedict and his monks to the oratory. The time had come for the daily praise of God, the public chanting of the Psalms.

"I'll go with you," said the Bishop. "It's a real tonic to pray with you and your brethren."

Although Benedict enjoyed meeting visitors, never losing an opportunity to help with their problems, he was really happiest when he could be alone. At such times he felt that God was very near. The troubles that so recently had bothered him now appeared for the flimsy things they were. But one day Benedict's solitary prayer did not furnish the usual joy. His soul could not shake off a mysterious sadness. Through God's grace, a brief vision had been granted him wherein he saw the trials that

SLOWLY, LIKE ONE IN A DREAM, BENEDICT
LOOKED UP AT HIS ANXIOUS DISCIPLE.

someday would plague the world. He heard the tread of millions of marching men. He saw bloody battlefields, weeping widows, orphaned children. He saw crafty men in high places, their hands heaped high with the profits of war. And he saw, too, that only a few people would dare to make his motto, "Peace!", their own.

The vision was such a dreadful one that Benedict could not control his tears. Presently, when Brother Theoprobus brought the news that some important visitors wished to speak with him, he gave no sign that he had heard. He remained kneeling by the window, his head bowed in his hands, his whole body convulsed with great sobs.

At the unusual sight Theoprobus rushed forward fearfully.

"Father Abbot, you've not had bad news from Brother Maurus?"

Slowly, like one in a dream, Benedict looked up at his anxious disciple. His face was twisted with grief.

"No, Brother. There is no bad news from France."

Theoprobus, a former pagan nobleman, owed his vocation to Benedict's preaching. For years, as a monk, he had enjoyed a close relationship with the Abbot. Now, seeing his beloved friend afflicted with some terrible sorrow, he decided to persist with his questioning. Perhaps there was something he could do to help.

"Please, Father Abbot—won't you tell me what's wrong?"

Slowly Benedict dragged himself to his feet. The

tears were still streaming down his face as he looked at Theoprobus.

"All this monastery that I have built, and all that I have provided for the brethren, are by the decree of Almighty God delivered to the barbarians!" he whispered weakly. "And I scarce was able to secure the lives of my monks."

Theoprobus stared in dismay. "Oh, no! Not that, Father Abbot! Surely there must be some mistake!"

Benedict smiled wanly. "There is no mistake, Brother. The passing years bring both good and evil fortune. The first is easy to accept. But the second? Ah, Brother—it takes a saint to understand misfortune!"

Chapter 21

THE END OF THE ROAD

A FEW weeks after this interview with Theoprobus, the day arrived for Benedict's yearly visit with his twin sister, Scholastica. Taking a few of his monks, the Abbot set out early in the morning for their customary meeting place—a house on the mountainside, halfway between Scholastica's convent and the monastery of Monte Cassino.

The Abbess had already arrived with a few of her community when Benedict came in the gate. There was a striking resemblance between the two, not only in physical features but also in dress, for the nun's habit was modeled after that of her brother, being a dark wool tunic with scapular and belt. On her head she wore a coarse black veil.

Benedict stretched out his hand in affectionate greeting. The Abbess Scholastica was his closest living relative. He had always had a deep love for this twin sister, but the fact that now they were the sole survivors of their family brought them even closer. Also, they were united in the service of God.

"Dear brother, I thought you'd never come!"

The Abbot smiled. "It's not like you to be impatient. What's the trouble?"

Scholastica sighed. "Nothing really, although lately I've not been too well. Benedict, do you ever feel that time is growing short? That one of these days we may be called to Heaven?"

"Sometimes. After all, we're not young any more."

"Sixty-seven years old!" mused the nun softly. "That's a good lifetime."

Benedict nodded. During these sixty-seven years, from 480 to 547, much had happened in Italy. The barbarians, Odoacer and Theodoric, had ruled for the greater part of the period. Then, in 535, the Emperor Justinian had invaded the country, determined to revive the western Roman Empire and unite it with his holdings in the east. Just now King Totila was defeating Justinian's armies. For several weeks Rome had been in his hands. But he would not hold it long. Justinian would strike again, so that the long and costly war would stretch out to twenty years. Then would come a period of comparative peace, after which a new tribe of barbarians would invade the country from the north. These would be the dreaded Lombards— men destined to destroy the monastery of Monte Cassino in 581.

As the Abbot remained silent, Scholastica looked up curiously. "You're sad about something," she said slowly. "What is it?"

Benedict nodded. "I was thinking of our sixty-seven years," he replied. "Dearest sister, this sixth century is a troubled one. But its hardships are as nothing to those of the future."

Scholastica sighed. "You mean there will be more wars? More suffering?"

"Wars and suffering beyond belief, sister. Be sure of that."

The hours passed swiftly, with Benedict and Scholastica talking of many things. It was only in the late afternoon that they remembered to partake of the simple meal the nuns had brought with them from the monastery of Saint Mary. Tables were set in three different rooms—one for the monks, one for the nuns and one for the Abbot and his sister. As Scholastica served her brother, her heart grew heavy. Soon it would be time to say good-bye for another year. And she didn't want to say good-bye.

When the meal was finished, Benedict rose to his feet. Scholastica looked at him pleadingly. "Don't go," she begged. "It's not late yet and there are so many things to talk about."

The Abbot looked at the sky. "You wouldn't want me to break the Rule, sister. Don't you see that the sun is beginning to set? I cannot be away from the monastery at night."

The nun smiled. "You could dispense yourself. Just once wouldn't hurt. I'm an old woman, Benedict, with not much longer to live. Won't you do me this one little favor?"

"And give bad example to my monks?"

"Of course not. Let them stay, too. And my nuns. Oh, Benedict—let us hear you speak about God! Surely it wouldn't be wrong to spend the whole night in such a way!"

"The whole night? Sister! Do you realize what you're saying?"

"Of course I do. I'm asking you for a simple favor."

Benedict pushed back his chair. "There's just time enough for me to reach Monte Cassino and for you to be back at Plumbariola. Come along—walk out to the gate with me."

Scholastica made no answer. Joining her hands, she placed them on the table before her. A far-away look came into her eyes. Benedict watched a little uneasily. Was Scholastica praying?

As he was about to question her, a jagged streak of lightning cut across the heavens, followed by a crash of thunder that shook the whole house. From a sky cloudless a few moments before, torrents of rain began to fall. A strong wind came up, with great thunder and lightning. In all his years Benedict had never seen such a fearful storm.

Scholastica was undisturbed. She looked at her brother.

"Depart now if you can. Go back to your monastery and leave me here alone."

The Abbot stared. "God forgive you, sister! What have you done?"

"I asked you to hear me but you would not. I asked the Lord and He heard me."

For a moment the Abbot stood silent. Then, remembering his monks in the next room, he went to explain the marvel worked by Scholastica's prayers. When he returned, his face had lost some of its sternness.

"I guess you've won, sister."

"Then you will stay?"

"What else is there to do?"

Scholastica nodded. "Now I'll go and tell my Sisters about this great blessing."

The storm continued to rage. But the monks and nuns gathered about a large table scarcely heard it. The Abbot Benedict was speaking to them of the joys of Heaven.

As the hours passed, Scholastica's heart throbbed with joy. How good God was! He had heard her prayers and by His power over the elements forced Benedict to remain in her company. Truly, it was the best visit they had ever had.

"How well he speaks of heavenly things!" she thought, her eyes upon the Abbot's face. "He seems on fire with love!"

All present felt this, particularly the nuns, who had never before been privileged to hear Benedict speak at such length. What matter that they were going without sleep? It was a wonderful thing to hear the Abbot of Monte Cassino describe the beauties of Heaven. These beauties were so marvelous. What a reward for the hardships and sorrows of a few years on earth!

Toward morning the storm finally ceased. Birds began to sing and in the east the sun came up over a clean, cool world. Benedict looked at Scholastica.

"Perhaps I may go now?"

Scholastica smiled. "You have made me very happy. There's just one more thing."

"Yes?"

"MAY THE PEACE OF THE LORD BE WITH YOU FOREVER," HE SAID GENTLY. THEN, IN A LOW WHISPER: "AND ESPECIALLY WITH YOU, MY DEARLY BELOVED SISTER."

"Give us all your blessing, dear brother Benedict. And pray for us when you reach Monte Cassino."

Quickly the entire group of monks and nuns knelt down before the Abbot. "May the peace of the Lord be with you forever," he said gently. Then, in a low whisper: "And especially with you, my dearly beloved sister."

There were repeated farewells, then the monks and nuns parted company. As Benedict started out the gate, the Abbess turned for a last look.

"I wonder if he knows?" she murmured softly.

"Knows what, Mother?" asked a young nun.

Scholastica smiled. "That it's the end of the road."

The young nun was puzzled. "The end of the road? But we haven't started our journey. Our convent is down there in the valley. We have over a mile to go yet."

The Abbess nodded. "So we have," she answered calmly. "And likely our good Sisters are worried that we stayed away all night. Come along—we must hurry to set them at ease."

"Yes, Mother," said the young nun, but she continued to steal anxious glances at her beloved Abbess. *The end of the road!* What had the good soul meant by such strange words?

Chapter 22

BENEDICT'S LAST HOLY COMMUNION

TWO DAYS later the puzzle was solved. Sometime during the night, God had called Scholastica to Himself. She had passed away peacefully into that place of joy and beauty described so well by Benedict on the night of the storm. At once the nuns sent word to Monte Cassino, although the Abbot really needed no messenger to tell him of his sister's death. Once again God had given him the gift of vision. While at prayer, standing in his cell with his eyes uplifted, Benedict had seen his sister's soul in the form of a dove leave her body and penetrate the heights of Heaven.

"Another saint gives glory to God!" he rejoiced. Then he bade his monks go to the Monastery of Saint Mary and bring his sister's body to be laid in the tomb which one day would contain his own. The monks were a little surprised at such an order. Nevertheless they hastened to carry it out. In the oratory dedicated to Saint John the Baptist, which Benedict had built upon the ruins of Apollo's altar, Benedict's grave was made ready within the hour.

When the funeral procession finally arrived from Plumbariola, the Abbot was standing at the monastery gate. Almost the whole countryside had accompanied his sister's body to its last resting place. There were men and women of all ages, each with some little tale to tell of Scholastica's holy life. The nuns were silent, their coarse black veils draped over their faces, but the layfolk spoke freely. The Abbess had given bread to such and such a poor family and saved them from starvation. She had prayed for a sick child, and the little one had recovered in two days. She had found money to pay the debts of the poor. She had brought about dozens of conversions.

"Alas, what shall we do without her?" cried an old woman. "No one can take her place!"

Benedict smiled. "She will still help us," he said kindly. "And remember this, good friends. We have no reason for sorrow. Even as we stand here grieving because we have lost her, she is rejoicing in Heaven. If the Abbess could return to us—to me, her brother—she would not. Ah, my friends, why should we grieve because a friend of ours has gone to God?"

The funeral service did not last long. When Scholastica's body finally was laid to rest, the Abbot left the oratory and went to the upper room of his cell. He wanted to be alone for a little while—to pray and to think. This was the tenth day of February, 547. Deep in his heart he knew that his time on earth also was drawing to a close.

"Perhaps I'd better tell the brethren," he thought. "Then they can pray for me."

Some of the younger monks of Monte Cassino were not inclined to believe Benedict's prophecy that he would die in about five weeks' time—on the twenty-first day of March. But those who were older, who could recall previous wonders in the Abbot's life, felt he spoke the truth.

One morning Brother Theoprobus sought out his beloved superior. Ever since the day he had witnessed Benedict's great sorrow, had heard the tale of the approaching destruction of Monte Cassino, his heart had been troubled.

"Father Abbot, I'd like to ask you something," he said slowly.

Benedict smiled. "Yes, my son?"

"Our monastery is going to be destroyed by the Lombards in 581—in 34 years. You told me that some days ago. But could you tell me . . . that is, do you know . . ."

"Do I know if the monastery will be rebuilt?"

"Yes, Father Abbot. If only you could tell me that!"

Benedict nodded. "It will be rebuilt," he said kindly.

"And monks will continue to live under the Rule?"

"Until the end of time. Right now there is a seven-year-old boy in Rome who will do great things for our way of life. His name is Gregory. Some day he will be Pope. At his command, our monks will go forth to England and convert enormous numbers of people."

Theoprobus smiled. "Thank you, Father Abbot."

"There will also be nuns living under the Rule—as at Plumbariola," continued the Abbot. "They will be found in all parts of the world, helping the poor and sick, educating children. There will be Oblates, too—inside our monasteries and out in the world, men and women who love our motto, *Peace.* Many of them will become saints. All of them will do what they can to make our way of life known and loved."

Theoprobus was silent. In his mind's eye he was seeing the Abbot's prophetic words come true. It was a solemn moment. Yet this glimpse into the future gave cause for joy. The way of life Benedict had laid down for his followers—monks, nuns and Oblates—would be followed until the end of time! It would be found even in distant lands!

The weeks passed. On the fifteenth day of March, Benedict gave orders for his grave to be opened. A little later he took to his bed with a high fever. Although his older followers realized that this was the beginning of the end, the younger monks continued to hope. Their good Abbot had worked so many wonders for other people. Why couldn't he work one for himself? A man of sixty-seven years really was not old. Many saints had lived to a far greater age. Perhaps Father Benedict would do the same.

"No," replied the Abbot faintly, as if reading their thoughts, "my work is done. Ah, brothers—pray only that it has been pleasing to God!"

With heavy hearts the monks went to the oratory

to open the stone tomb in which Scholastica's body had been lying for over a month. The brother and sister who had loved each other so much in life would not be separated in death.

"Perhaps something will still happen to keep him with us," said young Brother Mark hopefully. "Maybe we could find a new medicine . . . or perhaps, with proper rest and care . . ."

The others shook their heads. "Haven't you heard he will die in six days' time?" they asked, "that some of our brothers who are absent will see his glorious entrance into Heaven?"

Brother Mark nodded. "Yes, I've heard these things. But I was hoping against hope that we wouldn't lose our good father."

As dawn came of the 21st day of March, Benedict summoned his monks for the last time. "Take me to the oratory," he asked quietly.

Slowly the little procession set out, the Abbot supported by his sorrowing monks. When they reached the oratory, the monks wished to carry their beloved father to his customary place in choir. Here he could sit a while and rest. But Benedict wanted to be led before the altar to receive his last Holy Communion.

At the sight of such great love, some of the monks could not hold back their tears.

"Don't grieve," Benedict whispered, smiling upon his dear family as his strength ebbed. "I won't leave you alone."

Presently the dying Abbot received the Holy Eucharist. Standing in the oratory, strengthened

BENEDICT STRETCHED OUT HIS HANDS AND
BREATHED FORTH HIS SOUL IN PRAYER.

with the Body and Blood of the Lord, his trembling frame supported by his disciples, Benedict stretched out his hands and breathed forth his soul in prayer. Then, over a road strewn with carpets and shining with unnumbered lamps, he was seen ascending to Heaven.

New York City
Feast of Corpus Christi
June 24, 1943

MARY FABYAN WINDEATT

Mary Fabyan Windeatt could well be called the "storyteller of the saints," for such indeed she was. And she had a singular talent for bringing out doctrinal truths in her stories, so that without even realizing it, young readers would see the Catholic catechism come to life in the lives of the saints.

Mary Fabyan Windeatt wrote at least 21 books for children, plus the text of about 28 Catholic story coloring books. At one time there were over 175,000 copies of her books on the saints in circulation. She contributed a regular "Children's Page" to the monthly Dominican magazine, *The Torch*.

Miss Windeatt began her career of writing for the Catholic press around age 24. After graduating from San Diego State College in 1934, she had gone to New York looking for work in advertising. Not finding any, she sent a story to a Catholic magazine. It was accepted—and she continued to write. Eventually Miss Windeatt wrote for 33 magazines, contributing verse, articles, book reviews and short stories.

Having been born in 1910 in Regina, Saskatchewan, Canada, Mary Fabyan Windeatt received the Licentiate of Music degree from Mount Saint Vincent College in Halifax, Nova Scotia at age 17. With her family she moved to San Diego in that same year, 1927. In 1940 Miss Windeatt received an A.M. degree from Columbia University. Later, she lived with her mother near St. Meinrad's Abbey, St. Meinrad, Indiana. Mary Fabyan Windeatt died on November 20, 1979.

(Much of the above information is from Catholic Authors: Contemporary Biographical Sketches 1930-1947, *ed. by Matthew Hoehn, O.S.B., B.L.S., St. Mary's Abbey, Newark, N.J., 1957.)*

✠ SAINT BENEDICT ✝ PRESS

Saint Benedict Press, founded in 2006, is the parent company for a variety of imprints including TAN Books, Catholic Courses, Benedict Bibles, Benedict Books, and Labora Books. The company's name pays homage to the guiding influence of the Rule of Saint Benedict and the Benedictine monks of Belmont Abbey, North Carolina, just a short distance from the company's headquarters in Charlotte, NC.

Saint Benedict Press is now a multi-media company. Its mission is to publish and distribute products reflective of the Catholic intellectual tradition and to present these products in an attractive and accessible manner.

TAN·BOOKS

TAN Books was founded in 1967, in response to the rapid decline of faith and morals in society and the Church. Since its founding, TAN Books has been committed to the preservation and promotion of the spiritual, theological and liturgical traditions of the Catholic Church. In 2008, TAN Books was acquired by Saint Benedict Press. Since then, TAN has experienced positive growth and diversification while fulfilling its mission to a new generation of readers.

TAN Books publishes over 500 titles on Thomistic theology, traditional devotions, Church doctrine, history, lives of the saints, educational resources, and booklets.

For a free catalog from Saint Benedict Press
or TAN Books, visit us online at
saintbenedictpress.com • tanbooks.com
or call us toll-free at
(800) 437-5876